Gradually the World:

New and Selected Poems, 1982 - 2013

26 Aug 13
For Jim, fellow poet,
In friendship and with
affection and good wishes.

GRADUALLY THE WORLD:

NEW AND SELECTED POEMS, 1982 - 2013

BURT KIMMELMAN

DRAWINGS BY BASIL KING

BLAZEVOX[BOOKS]
Buffalo, New York

Gradually the World: New and Selected Poems, 1982 – 2013 by Burt Kimmelman
Copyright © 2013

Cover art, *Transition*, by Basil King
Interior art, drawings from *The Hudson River School* series, by Basil King

Art photos by Ani Berberian

Author photo by Diane Simmons

Interior design, cover design and typesetting by Geoffrey Gatza

Published by BlazeVOX [books]

All rights reserved. No part of this book may be reproduced without the publisher's written permission, except for brief quotations in reviews.

Printed in the United States of America

First Edition
ISBN: 978-1-60964-134-4
Library of Congress Control Number: 2013932522

BlazeVOX [books]
131 Euclid Ave
Kenmore, NY 14217

Editor@blazevox.org

publisher of weird little books

BlazeVOX [books]

blazevox.org

21 20 19 18 17 16 15 14 13 12 01 02 03 04 05 06 07 08 09 10

BlazeVOX

Also by Burt Kimmelman

Poetry

Musaics (1992)
First Life (2000)
The Pond at Cape May Point (2002)
Somehow (2005)
There Are Words (2007)
As If Free (2009)
The Way We Live (2011)

Criticism

The Poetics of Authorship in the Later Middle Ages: The Emergence of the Modern Literary Persona (1996)
The "Winter Mind": William Bronk and American Letters (1998)
The Facts on File Companion to 20th-Century American Poetry (2005, Editor)
The Facts on File Companion to American Poetry (2007, Co-Editor)
William Bronk in the Twenty-First Century: New Assessments (2013, Co-Editor)
Machaut's Legacy: The Judgment Poetry Tradition in Late Medieval Literature (forthcoming in 2014,
    Co-Editor)

Acknowledgments

Gratitude to the publishers and editors of these journals and anthologies in which some of these poems have appeared, at times in earlier versions: *Apostrophe, Backwoods Broadsides, Big Scream, BlazeVOX, Body, The Brave Little Poem of the Day, College English Notes, Confrontation, The Cortland Review, The Cultural Society, Dead Owl, EOAGH, First Intensity, Future Cycle Poetry, Golden Handcuffs Review, Hamilton Stone Review, Home Planet News, House Organ, Jacket, Light & Dust Anthology, Lips, Little Red Leaves, Marsh Hawk Review, Moria, Mudfish, Muse Apprentice Guild, Napalm Health Spa 2012, New America* (New York: Autumn House Press, 2013), *The Newark Review, The New Promised Land: 120 Contemporary Jewish American Poets* (New York: Continuum Press, 2013), *On Barcelona, The Phoenix, Pequod, Poetry New York: A Journal of Poetry and Translation, Poetrynow, The Poetry Superhighway, Poets Online, Poets USA, Rampike, ReVisions, The Second Word Thursdays Anthology* (Treadwell, NY: Bright Hill Press, 1999), *Segue: A Journal of the Arts, Shofar: An Interdisciplinary Journal of Jewish Studies, Shot Glass, Sub Voicive Poetry, Sugar Mule, Taj Mahal Review, Talisman: A Journal of Contemporary Poetry and Poetics, Truck, The Trumpeter, Tuesday; An Art Project, Verse Daily*, and *The Writer's Almanac*.

Profound thanks are also extended to the publishers and editors of these books by Burt Kimmelman:

Musaics (New York: Spuyten Duvil Press, 1992)
First Life (Jersey City, NJ: Jensen / Daniels, Publishers, 2000)
The Pond at Cape May Point (East Rockaway, NY: Marsh Hawk Press, 2002)
Somehow (East Rockaway, NY: Marsh Hawk Press, 2005)
There Are Words (Loveland, OH: Dos Madres Press, 2007)
As If Free (Jersey City: Talisman House, Publishers, 2009)
The Way We Live (Loveland, OH: Dos Madres Press, 2011).

Cover art, *Transition* (Library chalk and Higgins ink), by Basil King.
Interior art, drawings from *The Hudson River School* series (Higgins ink), by Basil King.

Art photos by Ani Berberian.

Author photo by Diane Simmons.

For Diane and Jane, as always

> *Tot iorn meillur et esmeri*
> *car la gensor serv e coli*
> *del mon....*
>   — Arnaut Daniel

CONTENTS

New Poems, 2011 - 2013 21
    Lips 23
    Early Morning, Sea of Marmara 24
    Cup of Tea, 5 AM 25
    After the Rain, Autumn 26
    Train to Izmir 27
    El Paseo 28
    First Hot Day in April 29
    York Beach, Maine, Early Morning 30
    Afternoon, Istanbul 32
    Early April Awakening 33
    Jerry Orbach, Dead Today 34
    Early April Dawn 35
    Sparrows After the Rain 36
    Los Angeles, Getty Museum 37
    Red Maple Tree, Mid April 38
    November Dawn 39
    Zydeco 40
    Blue Jay, Sun 41
    December Solstice 42
    After Rain, October 43
    Mid March Morning 44
    A Visit to Gloucester 46
    Marriage 47
    The War Is Over 48
    Istanbul 49
    Café, New Year's Day 2005 51
    "Samuel Menashe, New York Poet of Short Verse, Dies at 85" 52

Poems, 1982 – 1992 53
    Tate Gallery / Gaudier-Brzeska's Pound, the *Hieratic Head*, 8.6.86 55
    Of Poetry II 56
    Franz Marc's *The Fate Of The Animals* 1913 / Boston 1991 58
    Making the Bed 59
    Miró At The Guggenheim, 8.13.87 60
    Gerstl's *Two Sisters*, Vienna 1905 / Museum Of Modern Art 1986 61
    Zeus in August 63
    Kandinsky's *Winter Landscape* 1910 / Fogg Museum 12.300.87 64
    The Argument 66
    7/27 One Block from *Notre Dame* 67

Motherwell's *Sepia Elegy* / Museum Of Modern Art, 1.4.88 68
The End Of Nature 70
Anyone We Know 71
Charles Demuth's *Blue Nude* 1913 / Whitney Museum 1.8.88 73
7.31.86 Degas' Dancers 74
Musée Rodin, 8.1.86 76
Fourth Of July, Fire Island Beach 79
1.31 Moravia, New York 82
The Fabric 84
Musée Picasso, 7.28.86 85
The Ox Pull 86
5.2.87 Waiting For Diane At The Klee Show / Museum Of Modern Art 88
First Life 89
Doisneau's *Ballade Pour Violoncelle* 90
First Year 93

Poems, 1993 – 2002 97

For Jane, Age Three 99
Autumn 100
Letter to My Dead Brother 101
Waking Up 102
Flagstones 103
Xmas Tally 104
Late February Sun 105
Getting Ready 106
Jane and Ryan at the Shore 107
Waking My Daughter for School 108
Lying in Bed with My Daughter 109
The Pond at Cape May Point 110
Pine Tree 111
Rain 112
Geese 113
Afternoon Haze 114
Feeding 115
Swirl of Water 116
Dawn 117
Morning Pond 118
The Wind 119
After the Storm 120
Sudden Noise 122
Hunting 123
Bath 124
Scrub Pine 125
Early Morning at the Pond 126

Intruders 127
Wounded Bird 128
Whatever 129
Daylight 130
Egret 131
Morning Light 132
Squall 134
The Swan Looks Backward 135

Poems, 2003 - 2011 ..... **137**
Somehow 139
Sol Lewitt's *Double Pyramid* 140
The Evening 141
Standing Stones 142
The Assumption Of Matter 143
Yellow Flower 144
Self-Portrait 145
Sidewalk Café, Spring 146
Late October Rain 147
Gerhard Richter's *Stag* 148
Somewhere 149
Late in a Slow Time 150
Taking Dinner to My Mother 155
Blackeyed Susan 158
Fra Angelico at the Met 159
Poem for Jackson Mac Low 161
Tuft of Lavender 162
Raking the Leaves 163
That Boy 164
"Queen's View" of Loch Lomond 165
Plan 166
The Coming Snow 167
Ed Ruscha's *Course of Empire* 168
Susan Sontag Has Died 170
Seasonal 172
Old Age Home 174
Cicadas, July 175
Richard Pousette-Dart's *Night Landscape*, 1969-71 176
Start of Day 177
Crumbs upon the Table 178
Two Blackbirds 179
Perhaps Starlight 180
Three Women Smoking Cigarettes 181
The Sleep of the Dead 182

Home from the War	184
Washing My Brother's Hair	185
Late February Snow	186
Café in Maplewood	187
Summer's End	188
Edvard Munch's *Despair*, 1892	189
Friends Gone	190
Brighton Beach, August	191
Gust of Winter Wind	192
Getting Old	193
Abandoned House	194
After Robert Creeley	195
Birdfeeder	197
The Sapling	199
Big Wind in a Small Town	200
Start of Spring	202
Hameau de l'Eglise 8.25.05	204
Early March Afternoon	205
The Seeds of the Red Maple	206
Lido Cristoforo Columbo	207
The Cardinal	208
Variation of Green	209
Visiting the Nursing Home	210
Laocoön and His Sons, Museo Vaticani	211
"I Feel a Song Comin' On"	212
Neighbors	213
The Deception	214
House, Normandy	215
Snow Shine	216
Bar Mitzvah	217
On Raccoon Ridge	218
Tilted Arc	219
The Waves	221
Monet's Garden	222
Jane Planting Flowers	223
Marlene Dumas' *The Kiss*, 2003	224
Late January Morning	225
Alhambra Steps	226
Mikvah, Warsaw Ghetto 1941	227
Big Storm	228
With Fred Caruso, Standing in Front of Pierre Bonnard's *Corner of the Dining Room at Le Cannet*	229
On a Terrace, Waiting to Enter *El Palacio Nazaríes, Alhambra*	230
Cicadas, Mid July	231

Stone Love 232
Summer, Young Woman by the Westside Drive 233
The Way We Live 234
Wild Onions (After Robert's Letter) 236
Robin, Spring 237
Late November in the South Mountain Reservation 238
Domestic 239
At a Willem de Kooning Show with Michael Heller 240
Storm, Beach, Gull 241
Looking through the Picture Window at Poets House 242
Early April Morning 243
Arctic Terns 244

Praise for Burt Kimmelman **247**
   About the Author 252

so different from all maps

— Susan Howe

Gradually the World:

New and Selected Poems, 1982 - 2013

New Poems, 2011 - 2013

Lips

I shave my face and think of how this act,
in the eyes of a boy, is what makes him
a man, this ritual, the razor's edge
scraping skin and a careless cut welling
blood, this strange pleasure. I pull my cheek taut
with a fingertip, then examine my
contorted mouth. I see there my father's
lips, for a moment, thin and primly closed,
and my mother's full lips, parted slightly
to say something against his indifference,
perhaps, only to think better of it.

Yet somehow in the mirror my lips are
my own, even with my parents' faces
before me, and their delicate mouths most
of all, as they were when, a small child,
I used to look up at them, listening
to what they were saying to me. Now their
words are my words, this poem, their kisses,
too, my kisses, come of that union long
ago. I never saw them kissing, though,
never an embrace, and in their old age,
I with a daughter, they perished apart.

I found my dead father, his head resting
on a pillow, in his death mask his lips
wrenched sideways, twisted as if, in wanting
to utter a final thought, he had sought
an elusive breath of air. My mother,
dead, was held in a dream of a deep lake,
one morning in her bed, a dried trickle
of blood at the corner of her mouth, her
lips joined in the fullness of silence. What
in the end did I owe them but to leave
them each a final kiss on their cold flesh?

Early Morning, Sea of Marmara
January 2012

Clouds over the dark hills,
birds in twos and threes cross
the water as slowly

as the ships below them,
float on air — on their way
through the streaks of new light.

Cup of Tea, 5 AM

No reason
to wake up
early, no

light yet in
the window —
only that

the day has
begun though
in darkness.

I switch on
the kitchen
lamp, set the

flame under
the kettle —
later sip

my tea, hot
and harsh, and
watch the dawn.

After the Rain, Autumn

Blue flowers bow
over the walk
after rain — leaves,
too, have fallen.

Train to Izmir
January 2012

Low hanging cloud cover,
plowed fields, squat trees, crouched stone
station where we enter
a town, electrical
lines, satellite TV
antennas, a distant

minaret, hills either
side of the platform, grave
markers among tall grass,
a circling river, bridge
over it, half-built
homes nearby — we peer in.

El Paseo
>Festival of the Three Kings
>Barcelona, 5 January 2011

The brightness of solstice evening
and the procession of tableaux
through the street, the night of the Three
Kings, and the only way to get
from here to there is underground
where musicians play songs hundreds
of people stop to sing before
their trains arrive to take them home.

But Diane and I veer away
to *La Rambla*, even tonight,
for our *paseo* before
dinner, the crowds here on the move,
many people arm in arm as
they walk, above them white lights strung
in trees that front the buildings' stone
facades along the grand boulevard.

The cafés are everywhere, chairs
and tables and diners, and
mimes in their costumes portraying
the fascinations of our lives —
later we stroll through a courtyard
by a church where there are people
admiring a Christmas crèche —
the day's siesta long over.

First Hot Day in April

Tulips reach
for the sun,

petals splayed

wide apart
in ecstasy.

York Beach, Maine, Early Morning
26 June 2012

Slate gray water, white
spray on waves, foam left
on shore, dark cloud stretched
across the vast sea,
I think of that far

edge where I must end —
and there the lighthouse,
a black rift in dawn,
perpendicular,
joining earth and sky.

Afternoon, Istanbul

Gulls bob on water, bask
in sun — ships too, not far
off the Marmara shore,
waiting their turn to move
up through the Bosphorus,
then into the Black Sea.

Early April Awakening

Green bamboo
leaves wave in
front of the

white cherry
blossoms and
behind them

the maple
tree in mid
morning sun.

Jerry Orbach, Dead Today

"Jerry Orbach, Star of 'Law & Order,' Dies at 69"
- *New York Times* 29 December 2004

Not so strange how
a person comes
to an end, the
body simply

giving out — though
the world goes on,
and we sometimes
might even think

of it without
us, a summer
evening, let's say,
at an outdoor

café, people
talking over
drinks as they cleave
to the late light.

Early April Dawn

New light turns the sky
gray and then the start
of blue — the small leaves
on swaying branches
the color of earth

below. I have come
back to bed, teacup
in hand, having fetched
the *New York Times* from
my front walk where it

was tossed in the night
from a passing car
whose headlights made plain,
for a moment, what
should have been left as

it was. I lay down
my paper to look
for the dawn — a bright
spot from my reading
lamp in the window —

behind it vague trees,
a house, the mute night
though a few birds up,
somewhere beyond their
quick chirps just begun.

Sparrows After the Rain

Sparrows in puddles
after the rain — wings,
drops of water — rise
up all at once, fill
the air as I pass.

Los Angeles, Getty Museum

White tram to the top
of the mountain, palm
and cypress, cactus —
the city, its heat,
left below us —

in the pavilion
white stones, water spouts,
fountain of jagged
rocks, people talking
in the breeze, drinking,

a young woman, hair
floating like the girl's
in the Klimt poster,
swings herself around
a pole in the sun.

– 21 July 2012

Red Maple Tree, Mid April

If more seeds fall
will I learn the nature of rain?
— Rachel Blau DuPlessis

Swaying in air
below the branch

a filament
of the tree's red
flowers, soft pulp

caught in a silk
thread — the weeping
spring, the letting

go to begin
again — the earth

embraces all.

November Dawn

I wake hard grasped, quivered alive
— William Bronk

The slow light returns
so I take my first
steps, with care, make my
way down the dark stairs
in the thin gray dawn.

I fill the kettle
and set the stove's flame,
head out the front door
where the newspaper
was tossed in the night.

With my cup of tea,
back in bed, I read
of sorrows and joys,
think of the day, what
there is to be done.

Zydeco

They take their time setting up —
the fiddler chanting in her
microphone "one two one two,"
the guitarist fingering
his strings, twisting pegs to get
tuned — the crowd starting a new
round of drinks, having eaten.

The accordionist starts
to play and the dancers take
the floor in a slow two-step,
later a waltz — some twirling
and prancing but mostly they
hold close to one another —
so to hold to the music.

She feels for his step as they
circle the others — his hand
firmly on her waist, her
head tilted forward a little
in her pleasure — everyone
swaying to the bassist's beat,
the singer's rasping Creole.

        Rosendale, New York
        4 November 2012

Blue Jay, Sun

> *thru birdstart*
>   – Lorine Niedecker

Blue Jay screaming its signals
among leaves as I come near

— blue in green, crest up, sunlight —

hops to the next branch, screaming
at my striding underneath,

ascends to the treetop, screams
once more as I pass below.

December Solstice

Night's dream lets go slowly —
at once bare black branches
in the window, behind
them the white house across
the way, in the first gray
light of dawn, the new day.

After Rain, October

Purple asters fall
on the walk after
rain — wet leaves, too, have
dropped, bereft of home,
stuck to stone, to dirt.

Mid March Morning

Small red buds
on the bare
branches, sun,

blue sky, not
a cloud — from
the tree top

a bird flies
off, something
in its beak.

A Visit to Gloucester

> *I take SPACE to be the central fact to man born in*
> *America, from Folsom Cave to now. I spell it large*
> *because it comes large here. Large, and without mercy.*
>   – Charles Olson

I look out on the vast, flat sea
from hills behind a bog winding
down to a sandy inlet, shore
beyond it, open to the sun —
and now know why space is the fact
of our lives and why, a large man,
he needed a large page to write
that language, an unkempt story.

Scratched into a notebook or scrawled
on the walls of his apartment,
the words inhabit a place, find
the will in ocean, continent —
set directions from the harbor
for "islands hidden in the blood"
or, water at his back, the peopled
land glimpsed "from this place where I am."

    2 July 2012

Marriage

> *For you*
>
> *also (also)*
> *some time beyond place....*
> — Robert Creeley

It is just
what you would
not think, that

somewhere there
is a plan
gone wrong (kept

off balance,
catching up
and breathless).

The War Is Over

I meet my friend, my old professor, and we head over
to Zuccotti Park, lots of cops and metal fences on the way
there, and then the drums in sync, and dancing and signs —
scrawled on a piece of green cardboard, "Compassion
is the radicalism of our time," set up against some
empty pizza boxes, and another sign, photo of grave
stones below the heading "No Corporations Buried
Here" and below the graves "Arlington Cemetery" —
and then I see a young man and young woman cuddling
in a sleeping bag in the middle of it all, trying to rest.

We two old lefties head off to catch our trains back home,
and it's then I remember that heady day when, out of nowhere
someone starts chanting "The War Is Over," 1968 in Washington
Square Park, and thousands of us pick up the chant, and then
we start marching up Fifth Avenue and shouting "The War Is
Over, The War Is Over," Allen Ginsberg and Gregory Corso
somehow having ended up at the front of the march, and I see
two old timers beside us on the sidewalk as we pass them by,
as we march by, and they're shaking hands and laughing, telling
one another "Hey, the war is over," and patting the other
on the back in their glee, and in the street we all are headed
uptown, tens of thousands of us now, and the police have just
arranged themselves alongside of us and they're letting it all
happen, and when we get to 42nd Street, Allen taking half
of us west to the Hudson River, Gregory the other half
to the UN and the East River, and we all knew what happened.

I wait for the hundred thousand of us to start marching from
that downtown little park, heading north, cheering and protesting,
and in DC and in all of our cites, and I'll be there, since now's the time.

Istanbul

On Galata Bridge

Late sun lighting houses
on the hills of Asia
crouching by the water —

we cross the Golden Horn
among thousands on foot,
in trams or cars, passing

men who bait and cast their
lines below — muezzins' calls
behind, ahead of us.

Ferry on the Bosphorous

We press onto gangplanks,
head to our seats, order
tea, the gulls following

the boat across, outside
our windows minarets
and domes, hills and water.

Tea in the Grand Bazaar

City of passageways,
lights of lamps, jewels, rugs,
meat roasting, spices — one

way, another — we stroll
along in the crowds, young
men cutting through, their

trays of tea for people
in their shops, curved glasses,
each with its tiny spoon.

Early Morning

Clouds over the dark hills,
birds in twos and threes cross
the sea as slowly as

the ships below — the train
coming by, cars hugging
the shore — day beginning.

Café, Blackout

We sit by the wood stove,
reading by candlelight, sip
tea until the music,

slow and sobbing, comes back
on — a man smoking his
hookah in time, long pulls

of smoke, then the muezzins'
prayers broadcast through the streets,
announcing the evening.

Sea of Marmara

Light across the water —
far off a ship waiting
its turn to steam into

the Bosphorus — on shore
a man rests on a park
bench, watching the dark sea.

Café, New Year's Day 2005

"Huge Quake Spawns Tremors and Tsunamis in Southeast Asia"
— *New York Times*, 26 December 2004

January sun
is a haunting thing,
and the various
people, whatever
talk is left over

from the night before
filling in the room
along with the hiss
of the espresso
machine, sip coffee,

maybe eat a bit
of bread and not much
else, and watch the light
of the late morning
cover the tables

nearest the picture
window, then dissolve
into the dark street —
the catastrophe
an ocean away.

"Samuel Menashe, New York Poet of Short Verse, Dies at 85"
New York Times, 23 August 2011

> *Your ashes*
> *In an urn*
> *Buried here*
> *Make me burn*
> *For dear life. . . .*
>   — Samuel Menashe

Words let us
live — so you
read them twice,

your voice for
good measure,
though you knew

how silence
could make them
beautiful.

Poems, 1982 – 1992

Tate Gallery / Gaudier-Brzeska's Pound, the *Hieratic Head*, 8.6.86

His eyes look at no one, and looking,
we turn away from the broken, the human passion,
to form in a sublime dream, unreal, apex
in some space somewhere. Whoever walks through

the gallery's high marble archway sees his head, solitary
and solemn, very center of the room and sky through windows;
this is Gaudier's cold aspect, folded skull
at once homeric rigor though something still undone

and possibly dangerous. Is the mountainous forehead
proud? Perhaps. Yet in outright and unforgiving denial
of tenderness, the imperfect, fallible, to find some
remote idea, star, or other imagination: a shape of flesh

covers the alien bone and the seeming lower lip disappears,
we might think bitten softly in contemplation between
invisible teeth, and a hard jaw set thinking the impossible.
We are unforgiven and denied, in our absolute terror

amazed at what arc crosses the absolute stars. There is
a draft of sunlight. A hand passes along and over
a heavenly shape, and as it feels carefully this hand finds
mute stone.

Of Poetry II

for William Bronk

If there is only the work, as you say, and
there is
only this, then
let's not speak of it, after all, and
listen to it.
for in the light of

the summer day and the flat
ground
and hills where we are bound
we might

draw the world with us in it, call
to that boundary, and

where we are, yet
we're drawn
to it, to that thing . we

are

here

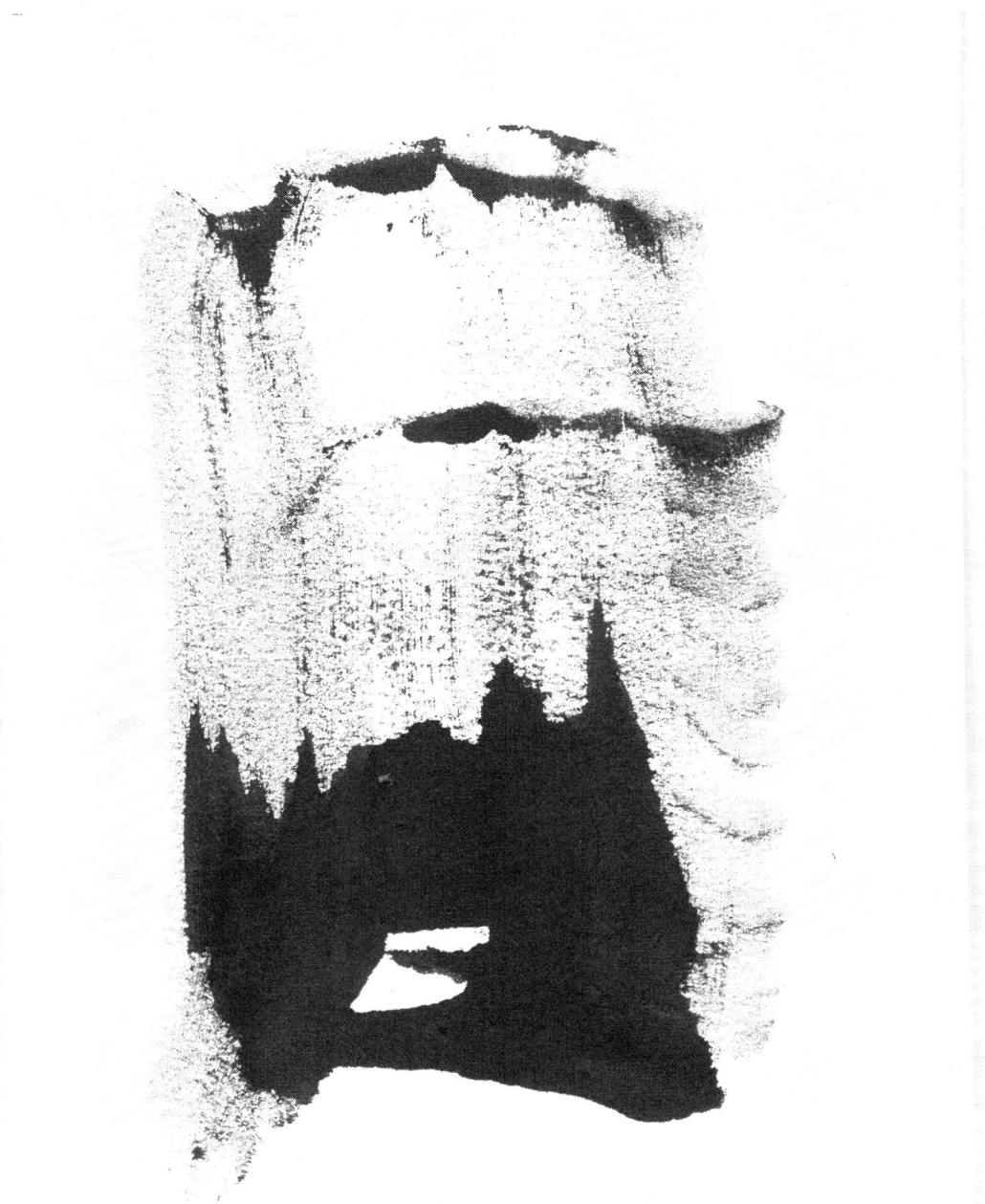

Franz Marc's *The Fate Of The Animals* 1913 / Boston 1991
Seth Kimmelman, 1951-1991

Among the dangerous shards
the breathing animal turns,
nervous and bright, and looks
into the dead wind. The act

is simple — yet, the world's
structures abandoned, to find
a place in the wreckage
incalculably complex. You

lie on your couch in your
"living room," your useless
spindle legs rest on my
visitor's lap. What will

become of us all, living
and dead? You say it's not death's
mystery but the details
of disaster, the new

illnesses each day, which
overwhelm — and the sane
tubes, their clear liquids, their
unforgiving order; they

are sleepless, without any
musculature — they are
here while you, incredibly,
disappear before our eyes.

Strange enough, there's no longer
confusion. We speak softly,
brother to brother, now
of all the things we'll miss.

Making the Bed

for D.

summer country. in the morning the leaves
bend

to the window & fold
the house in . mountains & sun . i fold

the blankets, hand smooth. When
you're here

i know it. The sun crosses

the hand's breadth —

& in your face

the unenterable
image. Under

your eyelids
night unfolds. Pull

the blanket over you
and with it

the evening air .

Cummington, Massachusetts, August 1988

Miró At The Guggenheim, 8.13.87

the hair line
across

the eye, the red sun, these

are the creatures
of the air

who dance and cajole . these things are

to be loved, sight
to which we cling

as precious filaments of

the blue
enormous sky .

Gerstl's *Two Sisters*, Vienna 1905 / Museum Of Modern Art 1986

They're unlike each other and the same,
sitting together, looking out

at us —

hands and feet
hidden under white frill dresses,

the white edges
escape into full black canvas

behind them. One sister's a bit younger,
and beautiful, her neck

disappears into satin
and lace below holding

the line of her, her jaw and eyes,
smooth skin, round, and the thin even

cut of the lips keeping
a girl's curiosity:

how little

the sisters say to us who see them, comfortable,
quietly well fed. They've seen the new universe

through their window, its light
covering their faces with the late afternoon.

They'll see the stars
as if through a gauze curtain,

the maps romping and whirling,
early evening lamp

against the beyond, soft light
and white lace, parlor. They

sit so still, eyes the same,
black, round, telling us nothing,

the world

expressionless and open — we look in
who are so bloody, unrested.

Zeus in August

we'll mambo through the thickest
nights

you
many bellied from children
you pained for

i stick to your wet breasts
drink your wet thighs

Kandinsky's *Winter Landscape* 1910 / Fogg Museum 12.300.87

The white
of the snow

belongs to
the wind

and the man . One leg
the other

down to soil
asleep

below
the white blanket . a stone wall

holds
the field in, and

to the other side
the town beyond

the wind
the roofs

and black mouths
turn this way

and that, the
dance. To walk

there. Home. Under
the blue daubs

of light
the flat

yellow sun
hangs and hawks

the darker places. The earth says
it dreams

when
the snow

keeps it warm, and the sun is in
its throat and shouts

to the raucous
sky .

The Argument

Something
we left
unsaid? The subway

speeds uptown
on steel wheels. When
will we

see
each other
again? I'll

be home. We'll
have something
to eat. We'll

come to the full
knowledge, your
tongue

in my mouth, one
of us inside
the other.

7/27 One Block from *Notre Dame*

> *Flurry of fat sparrows hits the fence*
> *top near the Oude Turfmarkt, whence*
>
> *look very surprised*
> *to have made it*
> *look around*
> — Paul Blackburn

A single block from *Notre Dame*, a little
after nine in the morning
single bell begins ringing   more bells
& more,   wide open
gray cool boulevard

picks up the sound of the tumble

through *la place* around
the cathedral front
other places automobiles in singles   doubles
in packs heading up the streets, & people too,
in twos & threes

birds circle it all   flocks of tens
twelves   fives or alone
— hold on tight to a cool wind

make much better time than the cars. paris

wakes up very slowly tho
the approach to *Notre Dame*
where I meet Stefan
is full of people around 8AM

tour buses, 3
mercedes limos full of japanese tourists *avec*
les appareils photographiques

But how not wake up slowly? last night
the sun went down at 9 thirty

Motherwell's *Sepia Elegy* / Museum Of Modern Art, 1.4.88

Nothing is ever decided. He looks at her
in the morning light where the hunger, the movement

is unmistakable, the bend of her hip & leg
when she sits — that joining

reminds him of
the corner of her eye

when she smiles — & this coming together
happens only in light, how it scatters

over the small rolls and ruts
of skin. In its power to make visible

the light will always be there, just as the skin
perishes

yet it's the skin
the soft skin

makes the light beautiful. He loves
the thought of it this way, this

touch of skin: what
he so remarkably sees becomes

the idea of warmth, light, this place
where he is, nothing beyond it. Here,

she says. He here
& she after all here. These any two things. After

all there's love, caress of flesh, touch
of the cheek warm as light. Her hair

his hair. Strokes of the brush
crossing so.

The End Of Nature

I tell you death, expect no smile of pride
from me. I bring you nothing in my empty hands.
  — William Bronk

There are integers, a life's breathing
in and out. The lead story in the paper
reads: "An End To Nature." Inevitable
reports of the known world falling through
the window of faith are said to be
plausible — sure as our hands or eyes.

In the blue clarity of the air
Augustine once read the world as if
it were a book in hand, at arm's length.
This grammar of sinew and bone is
still our only language — a celestial
bell severing the eternal night.

Rodin thought of hands, and shaped them, clasped,
ungrasping, one in the other. The day
folds into night — and then the unfolding
into the bright realm of the day star,
who rules mercilessly and forces
the marriage of earth and the pale moon.

Naked humans, small and frail, reach out
to the lighted world from within their
single certainty, *le main de dieu*.
This is the sculpted world, held against
the sky — the world in hand. There are counter souls
we think to call to, beloved, other.

Think of Yeats and his Dante. We are
our own *hic* and *ille*. What can I
name, what story tell my opposite
— unseen, a hand before my face? In
the vast museum I feel for you. Sightless,
we'll go the way alone, hand in hand.

Anyone We Know
Fernand Léger's *People by a Garden*
New York Metropolitan Museum of Art, 12.17.87

What will they think of us, those who come after, when they see us
so soundly simple, round and oddly opaque, each of our faces
and their lyrically

brutal, dependable bodies. Perhaps as we do they'll merely
look into the vacancy where we might, from Léger's garden, stare and
seem almost willing

to nod or smile. We never quite do, surprisingly, a little unready
to know something; we look out, beyond all seekers who would speak
to us. Unable

to see any thing outside our garden, we are left to think of ourselves
set so snugly in our home — as if to peer at ourselves within
the canvas and frame — for

this is indeed home, our sense of it
within the picture we own of ourselves. Though we look out
there's no asking

to see, really, the world, and without this outside we don't even
see us, never know us. Yet in the picture we glance out
to the real world

from round eyes, arms, unheaving chests — we can be
these broad proletarians who never decide the sure world where
there could be actual

light and shade, those all sensible differences, the unyielding distance
complete in its intent within itself and within the figures
it becomes. Just as easily

there's a passionate choice to admit carefully
in increments an examined world; this scrutiny, this shrewd seeing
is too a way

of feeling home. We know we can also deal out, with something like
tenderness, the non-choices, hold in balance massive unlovely
simple reds

blues, golds — torsos, arms and heads we come to own. As the seers
we are we can see how the tender parts we choose to love form Léger's
3 starers, each

fleshy mask, how the artist fashions a kind of fate in people
if he can, if in our belief we let him make us them. And if
we are them —

if we are unafraid and feel we can belong so close to home, flanked
and gathered by a few green leaves of plants each in its pot, to say
we are to each of us

without the possible garden
in our serene, bloodless terrain — sentenced
to the life-like

domain of the local — if we are them we will live here
quietly. As them we are strong and slowly recognize
we might be

willing to know anything if only there were a place we could reach,
the other, there, the one human twin, because from within the
painting of ourselves

where we find ourselves, the here that is there, there is only
the comforting horizontal and vertical — for Léger the black lines
you and I will always

name a window or shelf where light may come and pass. This
is the place we are given, from where we think to see more and where
each of us holds

the precious light against that day. Yet here is the made world containing
somehow much less than anyone ever imagines, where a machine of light
will lathe our hearts.

Charles Demuth's *Blue Nude* 1913 / Whitney Museum 1.8.88

She
is all

there is

her leg
out

the knee

& blue
naked

crotch

her arm
crosses

the blank paper

She
stirs

restlessly .

7.31.86 Degas' Dancers

the *jeu de paume*. squeezed into corners of the *salles*
off the main, squared hall, people and paintings,

impressionist crowds without sun or parks, lakes,
grassy fields & nude picnics, in woods by streams,
cool protective shade — all of this

is indoors, we collect around canvases, small sculptures
behind glass, wait other places, bustle or

rest along the outer promenade in wire chairs left every
which way, there & there, terrace in sunlight
above the tuileries, inside marble benches

at tops of stairs where we
mill about in french german italian english
spanish, bright blonde or dark sicilian

eyebrows over eyes or blankly back
either side. focus, thought, mouth
a little open and painfully amazed at all that beauty,

a *tristesse* against what we imagine
or remember later, that stillness
in the long gallery itself, the moment; we're in line

for tickets, in gift shop buy post cards,
in cafés we people manage half to say just

the wrong thing, never the certain perspective
an artist gives his intricate present,

here & now, color and movement . no south sea breeze
or boat on wavy blue parisian pond, sun,
sail, white . crazy red

& yellow air in van gogh's
little room, painted how many times? bed,
table, pipe, picture on wall. Yet particularly degas,

ballet, music in the painting . i'm
in a corner, in a canvas of 2 dancers —

he, kneeling, head back & looking up at her,
his arm reaches

to her waist to hold her, waiting, she,
one leg poised in air for grace, form

& balance, swings back out of
the far edge of her dancer's arc,

her pirouette caught up,
in & out of motion the two together. Movement. Long &

elegant, beside me, a woman, blonde, probably
german, eyes my dancers & maneuvers first
one leg through our corner

of the world, she — to step into
the next of the fabulous canvases, fables,
their lack of myth but fantasy

is everywhere, each brush stroke — steps lightly
past me without looking back

Musée Rodin, 8.1.86

Love is an agony. And here lovers merge in so many embraces,
all of them of
a piece of stone, a single idea:

the artist and his muse. He the *hand*

of god and also the human, perhaps broken, always
vulnerable being the hand holds

so to hold the world. There are other hands,
those which clasp only their opposites —

the sculptures of *the secret, the cathedral*.
All of these keep

the mysterious possibility, form itself; and like

the touching of *earth and moon*, or *night
and day*, we sense lovers hold themselves

like gods, that

because he was unafraid of myth he knew how
to translate the torment we see
in sinuous vein and flesh

into something
wild. So
the lovers of *eternal springtime* hold each other

in complete peace, uninterrupted
line and somehow a little unreal, and we see

in *the kiss*, as in all of his hands, that strength —
the unyielding in the lovers' need to grasp,

imprison a distance hands make their own. They startle,
vein and bone, long and huge,
as does his woman's long round belly.
But these hands and feet and faces are mortal,

easily damaged by unreasonable
inhuman natural forces like the sun,
wind, time most of all. *The first funeral*

tells us this in long hair and soft bodies folding
one over another — imagined rain in
an unstilled grief.

Everywhere,
in the house, garden beyond it,
there is measured time and space,

and a calm in the cool stone. Cool lovers.

I too move my naked
and immense hands and feet through
the old high wooden rooms and then out

into trees filtering summer sun onto
other forms, other statues outdoors,
and rest my long arm, as in *the kiss*, on a slab
of the unworked stone. There is a raw desire

in the cool but sunny day; thus I find
my way back into stone, its certainty.
The garden behind the house, its light

and shadows on statues bring memory out
with them into the brighter,

open air. In the museum itself
a woman sits sketching a woman
lying along her stone bed — on a bench
in the bright sunlight a woman lies beside

the figure of another reclining like a cat

stretches & sleeps again
in the sun.

They both look equally alive,
one asleep in flesh, the other

eyes closed
awake in stone.

Fourth Of July, Fire Island Beach

it seems the sun
never sets on this empire.
young thighs, red

as pomegranates,
and breasts heat up under
bikinis or sexy one-pieces — then cool

in water & foam.
wet hair
pulled back off bare ears

makes visible small
golden rings   .
           white sand stretches

off to infinity
or at least towards a bright haze where land
nestles with darker ocean   .   far to this sea

in silence
in which form is realized by a single
passing motor boat

a group of gulls
         sits bobbing
in the rolling ocean or else

two or three fly up
to an apogee & then dive
and swoop towards whatever is the new

feeding ground. One could —
i think - lose one's balance here,
the lovely lapse of memory

where reality occurs only
far out to sea (i was a bird
once

i was flying). the bathers,
especially the young,
seem to regain

equilibrium in surf & undertow
or eyes closed in the ever present
sand and sun slip

in & out of torpor .
the tumult of waves
plays up to the shore, drawing back

into unconsciousness of foam & tide
& green seaweed, the edges
of the mind

slightly undefined.   She
strolls
out of

the waves, her limbs are heav–
ier now,
her feet grip the wet sand, legs

and hips turning (and turning).
nothing stirs
while i am stirred

as if the world were in sync and motionless,
the living photograph of bright
blazing color — or is it myself

finally in step
with the sweep of the sea, the swoop
of the gulls, the step

of a girl?   young & bright,
she drifts by me
fluid in the middle

of world in suspension, all
light, color, the quiet
living memory . as

she passes she does not see me
there is only the sun

1.31 Moravia, New York

shred of sun in the afternoon
is the little death
in the snowy day.

watery light,
on the window, turns
and runs to ground. on the other side

of the world an invalid winter,
muffled winds on glass. deadwood,
bowed & descending

against a sky & along a hidden ridge in snow
& little winds, reminds us
of the light seeking

its own level,
turning inward & reflected
on the glass while turning

the afternoon, the flesh
of landscape,
visible and bare.

snowy gyres ranging
cross the hills. quixotes making war
in the sun ride furiously

over the crest & under & around the bones
of trees, white frozen dust in the sudden
remnant of light.

In the trap of evening
our light shines out: an empty face
in darkness. we see ourselves

in the objects of the day, their empty speech,
wood and snow, rise of land and trees
a map in wilderness. in the night

there are the stars, from another world,
voiceless: but it's the moon,
empty with light,

becomes the reflection
of our rawest
irrevocable form

The Fabric

What
we have left

undone, the fabric's
edge, threads

in air. Set up house,
chairs,

window, cover the bed
and table where

we sit — how not see you in

the morning,
any longer remember

the next day, the
next. Yet there

is an end to it —
the light in

the room, unraveled,
moving.

Musée Picasso, 7.28.86

Was this his house?
There is a broad courtyard full of white sun today, and high
stone walls — inside
the paintings and sculptures and scribblings must have been once
collected quite differently, half
women and bulls on canvases stacked
one behind the other, perhaps,
all eyes and breasts, shoulders,
and vaginas: here form

is understood in shattered hours, part icons,
sculptures gathered in
a room, a corner, facing one way
or another from each other yet not facing us
necessarily. Facing facing.

Among them now we read his biography
on the walls and the arranged
art-historical comments. Anyway,
who was this artist? We see
his paroxysm of labor — the work
is everywhere. When

did he ever find the time to fuck
all those women? There were of course
several wives with whom he must have fashioned
a kind of religious love-making, as if

his aching took him, without reason, elsewhere,
to a woman, and they
must have taken each other savagely and with

much care.

The Ox Pull
County Fair, Cummington, Massachusetts

The dark snout,
breath in cold air,

taut muscle, sleek skin,

sled of stone —

slide
and smooth the ground under.

The night

probes

not simply for

bruised flesh,
the weight of it. At the end

there is

the turn inward,
what can last —

the brutal struggle

to possess
fire and bear

the beating heart

in hand.

5.2.87 Waiting For Diane At The Klee Show / Museum Of Modern Art

If in the space
there are 2

lines, let one be
the wild happiness

the edge

measures . And if
there are faces,

we are
their round eyes,

or the hat   the foot

the finger   all the lighted
extremities

there . if
in the warm

light we must be

them, then we must
be

them. Let
the o

in oh you

mean we are
here

beyond
any form   .

First Life

for Jane

When you opened
your eyes you smiled

the doctor held
you at arm's length

your cord led back
where you'd never

return.
It took a while

before you cried
then you rested

and sucked. Later
you slept. What had

you seen in that
first instant — light,

movement. Somehow
in your strong voice

we knew it was
you, you who knew

voices — within
the dark, warm world.

The three of us
united

at the moment
of life.

Doisneau's *Ballade Pour Violoncelle*

But you — how slight — do
— Louis Zukofsky

    1.

Little hands
that hold mine —

ten months,
now you'll walk.

    2.

Rock

together

in the rocking chair, cool wind
3 A.M.

    3.

Above us
the solitary figure,

his instrument,

traversing Brooklyn Bridge.

    4.

Photograph
of the real

(Doisneau's
slight metaphor

in the strings).

       5.

Listen. There is
the empty street.

       6.

Each step

you turn.

Who's there?

Rock

to sleep,

pat my back,
little pats.

       7.

The wind, the towering

pylons

& cables

engulf the figure —

8.

as if

we're all alone,

each of us.

In sleep
the clear music

persists.

First Year
        Richland, Oregon

> *O loves of long ago*
> *hello again.*
> *all of us together*
> *with all our other loves and children*
> *twining and knotting*
> *through each other —*
> *intricate, chaotic, done.*
>   – Gary Snyder

Down "Sparta grade," the valley in sight

hills and mountains not unkind though bare

the gnarled shadows of 4 o'clock, slopes
and gullies, scattered sagebrush, snow on
the distant sky's edges — and below

always the desert, between corn and
alfalfa, flat bottom-land wet from

run-off; this year there's plenty of
water, but there are times when shovels
are used to fight off the "ditch-walker"

who regulates the flow, who turns back
the life force from some desperate farmer.

Before sunset we set out to cross

the near field of hay bales, Jane's birthday,

on her own, slipping on the pebbled
road that runs alongside, and chasing
some quail who strut ahead of us, just

out of reach, and then coming up on
the grass the flurry of shuttled air —

nested starlings, their trajectory
taking them away from us all at
once, wings, flutters, sudden awkward air —

and there are other birds: prairie hens,
jays, owls, robins, hawks, pheasant and grouse.

Here is what consolation there is,

all the old family gone, and we

the new "summer family" — *this* place,
the "home-place," the comfort to be had,
the mountains that are holding us in.

Jane struggles along and it's then that
Diane spots the brown and black smudge, and

adjusting our sight, in the tall grass
the breathing animal stops all three
of us, Jane pointing at what she sees,

the new fawn snuggling against the hay,
settled down deep, legs folded under.

Perhaps we learn by what's familiar,

the similar thing of families,

and in the family of children
one staring blankly at the other,
there's only the scent of the mother,

her call, but then the pull of the world,
its unforgiving complexity;

the breathing slows, standing still, Jane eyes
the deer's two black pools and two large ears
turned toward us to take us in, all three

— yet wait for the mother off somewhere,
the world, beauty, gathering itself.

In the intricate dance, sames and opposites,

it's best to follow "the center line,
with the out-flyers changing — fins, legs,
wings, feathers or fur, they swing and swim
but the snake center fire pushes through. . . ."

This is the first year of our return,
the turn back into soil of what's passed.

    7.20.91

Poems, 1993 – 2002

For Jane, Age Three

Saying goodnight is saying goodbye —
leave-takings are forever. When
you were born, time began — yet for you
there's no such thing as time.

I drop you off at nursery school,
the colors on the walls, the bright chaos
of finger painting, and cut-out shapes
of trees and people, these two dimensional

worlds without memory, lives lived
at odd angles. In roundabout ways
parents use I tell you we live in a world
of absolutes, the oddnesses not so remote.

For you it's simply instinct, the absence
and return. You pull my hair or let your
head rest in my arm; you ask questions,
questions. The asking, the beauty of talk

is something you've never had to learn.
There are times I say, "I'll always be back."
Strange, since you and I live with such
clarities, that dying has taken its shape.

Saying goodbye seems against all nature.
In this you've shown me the form of love.

Autumn

The cold comes without warning.

Nights, we close the windows —
turn on the lights,

the radio's music — outside
is the world.

Jane does her jigsaw puzzle. Her
small white hands

smooth over the fractures.
In the picture we look on.

No other moment,
we are alive

in the darkened landscape.

Letter to My Dead Brother

I suppose letters to the dead are common.
We need to speak, even when no one's there.
I think of the crazy juxtapositions, the people
and things you loved. Life is a mute grieving.

That's all I can ever say. I have a picture
of you holding Jane at six months, holding
her bottle to her mouth. She used to cry
to herself, a baby when her mother was away.
I'd become afraid. What could I do?

There are objects we inherit from the dead.
They make a strange language we speak
with astonishing clarity — we're surprised by it
yet there it is. The world, its textures, we cherish
them — we cling to them and live out the story.

You never learned how children keep our time.
They don't know us but our words, our faces
shape a world — and we, as if peering out
from behind it, understand how death forms
love, how the photograph becomes memory.

There is a connection that takes the place of
holding one another. I remember you when
Jane puts her arms around my neck. I feel
her warm breath, the blood coursing along.

Waking Up

Jane, you and I in bed
together, the fall
drizzle against the
windows — reds and golds

appear and disappear
in the wind. Like
the weather, we make
our unexpected entrances

and exits. There are
deaths autumn seems
to remember — the trees
bowing down, their

leaves below. My
address book is filling
up with useless
numbers. Never mind —

better not to move. The
floorboards creak if
we get up. Patiently,
Jane places each small

finger, one, another
between my lips.

Flagstones

The flagstones have been uprooted, branches
from underground and leaves scattered
in all directions. Today, after a fierce rain, stones
in the sun turn red and blue — shapes of water

disappearing.

Jane likes to lift the stones, to see the ants and
other strange creatures who burrow for a living. Their
legs, heads, antennae swirl erratically in a panic
of sensing — the loose wires of a civilization coming apart.

We look on.

Xmas Tally
Jane, Age Six

Sewing Kit

Thread the needle
then push it through

the thick cloth
and pull

Planet Kit

Once the paint dries
hang each globe

from your bedroom ceiling
by a thread

Drawing Kit

Thread the penciled color
across the page

Spell "thread"
Embroider your name

Bedtime

Kiss goodnight
(the thread of your breath)

Late February Sun
        Jane, Age Seven

The sunlight startles us awake,
loosens the ground whose shoots and buds —
their traces of red and blue — stand

against the odds. A squirrel makes
for her cache. The first woodpecker
rattles on, wrong yet beautiful —

no sense to the light, how we cleave
to its persistence. This morning
I also make for my cache of

papers, a pile of fallen leaves
on my desk, and instinctively
dig up this past autumn memo

from Jane: "cats birds dogs fish monkeys
whales dolphins." Her hand suddenly
sure and bright — why, though, no snakes?

I praise all creatures, who as if
they had never known winter are
now, too soon, desperately alive.

Getting Ready
Jane, Age Seven

Standing at the sink,
her fingers feel at
the strands of "hair" in
water, add shampoo,

rub and stroke — her smile
of concentration
says she's busy with
important matters —

the small doll getting
ready now to go
out into the world.

These rehearsals, these
evenings, her mother
on the phone, as I
pass the bathroom door

a moment before
nightgown, bed, book, then
covers overhead
to keep out the night.

Jane and Ryan at the Shore
Eight Years of Age

Legs curl under
in the darkened

sand. The waves run
easily up

the beach. Dolphin
fins pace the sea

beyond. Water
has found us all.

        Cape May Point, 1998

Waking My Daughter for School
Jane, eleven years old

I lean over your bed and kiss
your cheek. Everything that might
have happened — a night's tragedy —
has fallen away. Now, in the
moment, we are here together.

Your eyes open. You say "okay"
and sit up, looking around, it seems,
for a dream lost somewhere. You
dress for school, read the back of the
cereal box with your breakfast.

The early daylight overtakes
the kitchen lamp, gathering us.
How routine the day has become —
strange enough, as if it were meant
to be like this. Surely it is.

Lying in Bed with My Daughter

My half-grown daughter — old enough
to fend around the house — is sick
today, yet finds pleasure in this morning's
television carrying her
past the pain in her stomach. We
lie in bed together — I, in
her nausea, having given up
the day to a nervous leisure.

Slowly the warmth creeps up on us
and we, nodding off together,
forget the noise of busy lives.

The Pond at Cape May Point

Morning at the Pond

At the edge they poke
their beaks down

to pond bottom, its

muddy cache
of tendrils and worms,

then raise up

their heads to eat, look
around — drops

of water falling

back to the
sun's bright surfaces.

Pine Tree

From the ground
of fallen
pine needles
a leap up

flapping wings
to the tree's
lowest branch
hidden there.

Rain

The splashes and circles
in the water

among the shoots of grass
by the shoreline

signaling where to look —
a loose feather

floating among the swirls —
the tern places

first one leg, the other,
making her way.

Geese

The geese move steadily overhead,
their raucous signaling cutting short
the pond's quiet routine, and descend

together all at once, breaking the

water's plane in small splashes across
the wide curve of their crescent, float, look
around, and suddenly become still.

Afternoon Haze

Sky a single color —
and below, the trees thick

across water and sun —

shoots of bramble springing
up against the mud shore.

Feeding

Beak under
water, the

swan wags its

head back and

forth, tearing

the hidden
roots below.

Swirl of Water

Feathers up
in a fan,
the swan swims

after geese,
ducks — ousting
all creatures

from the swirl
of water
around her.

Dawn

The island — its rock
and bush, grass and moss —
in water's mirror

where algae and twigs,
weeds and mist, somehow
have drifted away.

Morning Pond

Circles in
the still shine —
wings overhead.

The Wind

Across the pond the tree
surges and twists as if

the sea, in agony,

or some other unkempt
creature, has come to stay.

After the Storm

Rain gone, the white flowers
on the brambles bow forward
over a mallard floating by
beside its image in the water.

Sudden Noise

Floating on the shadows of trees,
the far below current running
to the pond's deep center, the swan
turns his head toward the bank of sun
and sand — a sound already gone —
where, in a thicket of bramble
and blossom, some ducks are resting.

Hunting

Wings open
against
all winds,
the egret

rises up
over
its prey
then tumbles

far below
the bright
surface
of water.

Bath

Beneath the branch — whose leaves turn
the light askance among moss
and grass — the duck's bill searches
within the roughed-up feathers,
tugging at the wet and warm.

Scrub Pine

The humming
bird rises
slowly to
the branch of
pine needles.

The sparrow
hovers at
the pine tree's
topmost branch
then flies on.

Trees are wings
as they bow
to the sea's
salted wind,
standing there.

Early Morning at the Pond

Stuttering cheeps
All wings flapping
Heading away.

Intruders

The pigeons have landed on the island,
come down from the treetops
jutting into the sky
covering the far edges of the pond,

to settle for awhile along the skirt
of mud — grass, moss and rock
pacing the shore's image
in water — ducks, geese and swans gliding by.

Wounded Bird

Water covers
what it can
and makes the shore
where the bird,

wounded, standing
on its one
good leg, each day

finds within
the mud the life
of insects
to its liking.

Whatever

Torrents below,
untouched by light
or wind riffling
the pond's surface
and bending flight —

goose and swan, tern
and sparrow, test
the skirt of mud
for whatever
has lost its way.

Daylight

Above the treetops
the ducks descend
to the mirror plane

of daylight branching
within the shadows
keeping to the shore.

Egret

From seaward before the storm —
wings outspread over water
in slow, muscular movement —

the egret closes in on

the pond's far shore, touches down,
stands tall, enfolding itself,
its white oval silhouette.

Morning Light

Crocus
winding over
and over —

morning
light slides along
the current —

sleeping
birds under trees
on the shore.

Squall

Wind cutting
across water —
ducks turn their

backs, huddling
under pines
leaning in —

a gull floats
along, then
lifts itself

toward the sea,
leaving dark
deep behind.

The Swan Looks Backward

The swan looks backward when
it rests, head half tucked
under wing, then unwinds
its long neck into

its strange, precarious
arc, and on thin legs
ambles unsteadily,

lifting its skirt of
whiteness to the pond's edge,
and there among the
floating algae is still.

Poems, 2003 - 2011

Somehow

Somehow
though the cold
February

a bird
is singing
into the thin

early
light, its trill
then another

among
the branches
empty but for

the red
and blue flecks
incising the

day and
very soon
the riotous

raucous
gangs seizing
territory

so that
in this most
unforgiving

world their
insistence
is all there is.

Sol Lewitt's *Double Pyramid*
Whitney Museum Restaurant, 12.23.00

The other side of
the picture window,
its light borrowed from
above where the stone
blocks at street level

rest adjacent to
a hot dog wagon,
telephone booths and
people on their way
through the winter haze —

we hold whatever
glow there is, the clink
of dishes cutting
across the waves of
conversation, a

reprieve against the
dazzling colors on
the gallery walls.
How incredibly
lucky art is, its

shining like the sun,
undaunted — and we,
too, from below the
summit, in our odd
ways make it come true.

The Evening

Rub your leg
with mine, cricket, scrape
the dark heart and pull

on the night's
heavy gown.

Standing Stones
           Calanais, Isle of Lewis, Outer Hebrides

*The god commanded a naked stone be set up
and with no marks put upon it. But I had
lost that god or it had become something*

like a rain one hears but does not see.
– Michael Heller

At the top of the hill
the circle of ragged
stones among the moss, peat
and heather, and at its
center the burial
cairn where we fill our hopes
with a glimpse of the sun
here and there — I think of
the great night sky, the moon
without a cloud nearby
and silver picks of stars,
under which the deep silence
was marked by human voice.

The unworked stones standing
tall before the living,
found or quarried, raw and
yet so intelligent
in their perfect array —
how long since they were set —
oddly, they ignore the
aspiration toward grace,
the unforgiving crags
rough to the touch, having
made a space where time, a
mist, can come among us,
and then leave us in tears.

The Assumption Of Matter

The light at least was not to be dismissed.
— William Bronk

The newspaper tells us
what we come to know:
"New View of Universe

Shows Sea of Bubbles to Which

Stars Cling." At least until
more accurate sightings
from lensed outposts,

we see the world further from home,
come to feel more and more

our clinging selves
in the perfect stars.

Our galaxies
live
on surfaces

in a cosmos
twenty billion years old. And we peer in

to the patient emptiness. I
think of your poem
"The Annihilation

of Matter." We

do not
deny, dismiss

the light, Bill,

though we welcome darkness.

Yellow Flower

Rising up toward
the sunlight the

single yellow
flower holds out

its nectar for
the hummingbird

who comes only
rarely, on wings

— its flutter of
air and hooked beak

protruding, takes
what it's after.

        Tikal, 2004

Self-Portrait

I lean toward you
as if to say
here I am — not

my eyes or mouth

but this gesture
from the other
side of these words.

Sidewalk Café, Spring

Sun inside and out
of conversation,

across the walk the
sparrow hopping from

the building's shadow,
we gather in light.

Late October Rain

Water softens
the slight hold of
leaves on branches

bending over
with the weight of
autumn evening —

and the sun next
morning covers
what has fallen.

Gerhard Richter's *Stag*
        Museum of Modern Art, New York City 3.1.02

The blurred antlers,
obscure eye, taut
musculature —

the flat lines of
forest before,
after — half in

the hunter's sight,
lost in a world
without shadow.

Somewhere

Somewhere
in the dead
cold of winter

a bird
has begun
to sing. O when

does spring
begin its
slowest ascent?

Late in a Slow Time

Late January

White sun
across
branches —

windy
day, snow —
no one

believes
the light
will last.

Late February

No denying
the sun, even

in the moment
of cold, crocus

pushing through soil
into the world.

Late March

Streaks of light
cut across

the morning
ice, red buds

along the
simple brush,

a single
bird calling.

Late April

Blossoms then the leaves
among which a trill —
one note, another,
again — alights on
the scattered branches.

Late May

Light against
a bend of
leaves, birds half

in morning's
shadow, slow
heat rising —

several
peeps start up
all at once.

Late June

> *wave of warblers weaving*
> *chirp to chirp message*
> — Ronald Johnson

The day's signals, each warble,
trill and chirp, on again, off
again, on again, again —

once the red sun has seated
itself below the tree top
creatures cease their back and forth,

a sudden heat gone, slight breeze,
light tendering darkness — one
day, another, another.

Late July

The cicada
winds its plainchant
from earliest

daylight, scattered
like seeds below
the maple tree.

Late August

Warm sun all day
and the chill of

the evening moon —
its full face through

the tops of trees —
the leaves hold on

in the new dark.

Late September

Afternoon sun forcing
shadows under leaves, the
squirrels settle into
busy routines — running

along the limbs of trees,
digging in the warm grass —
already gathering

for the deep interval,
winter far off no more
to be denied in the
chilly dark of evening.

Late October

Red, pink, white
impatiens

growing wild
and tawdry

— half covered
with the fall

of leaves, sun.
No reason

it seems for
the cold air

— the late light
staying on.

Late November

The tree outside
my window is
bare now but for

one brown spot in
the vast slate sky,
a diffidence,

the brittle leaves
holding back what
must come to pass.

Late December

Thin ice along
the fragile branch

bending low of
its own weight, wind

and moon tighten
the new darkness.

Taking Dinner to My Mother

My mother sits on the edge of her bed,
a scarf on her head to hide the gray hair
she can no longer manage to dye black,
her flesh falling away from the frame of
her face and shoulders, loosened by the loss
of weight when the body betrays the soul,
when the body's pain forbids all desire.
But tonight she is hungry, and I have

come bearing corned beef and pastrami, bread,
sour pickles and a kasha knish.
I help her to the table in slow, small

steps, a *pas de deux* we have carried on,
I realize, for almost sixty years, and
I think of how, some time before, I held
my daughter's hands, bent over, as she learned
how to walk — the fact of balance, which we
live with until it abandons us — and
how my mother, in a photograph, held
me in the same way. Earlier today,

I had stopped at a café and, sitting
still for a moment, looking up from my
book, I watched how, at a nearby table,

a new mother fed her infant daughter,
who sat up in her baby carriage, some
bits of crustless bread held between thumb and
forefinger, while her grandfather talked on,
the smell of her mother's hand mingled with
this first food, a small bird in her nest. At
my mother's table I fix her sandwich
and tell her about her granddaughter who

met a boy for a moment in a flea
market, who is now a first love, but my
mother's eyelids are starting to lower,
her head nodding forward slightly, so I
gather her up and walk her back to her
bed, sit her down and swing her swollen legs
up and then under the covers, turn off
all the lights but one, close and lock the door.

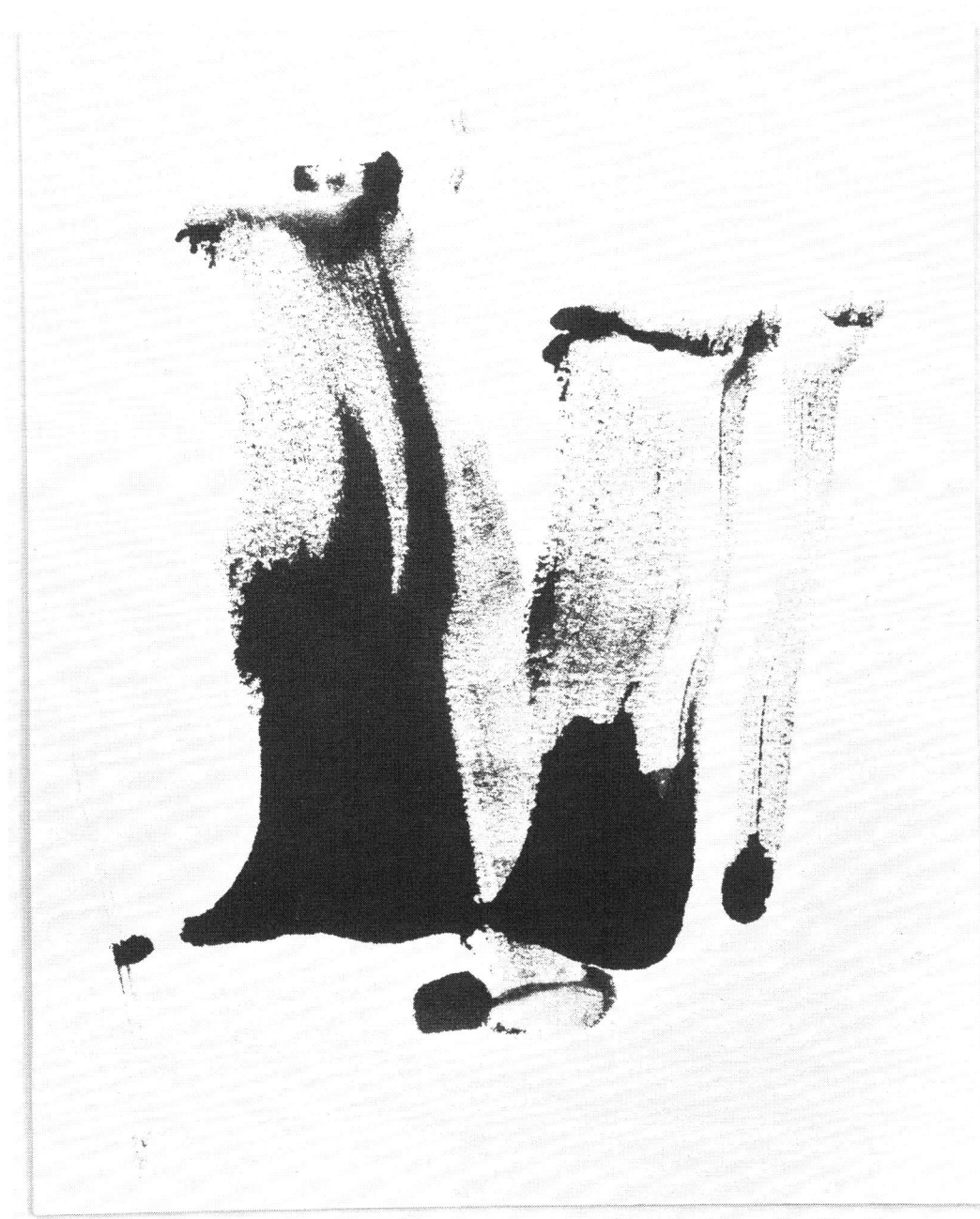

Blackeyed Susan

Blackeyed Susan, bright flower
in the sun, yellow petals
of late summer and your dark
heart of winter to come, you
bow ever so gracefully

over the edge of the trim,
newly cut grass, and let go,
in the breeze, your wild seed so
that, next year, there will be more
of you, and yet when you first

blossom we come to know the
dusk, how it settles in a
bit sooner each day, and how
you glow in the light you seem
to have stolen from the moon.

Fra Angelico at the Met
2 December 2005

The careful, golden light
holds them all — the wounded

supplicant, crooked leg and
bandaged foot, the rotund
cleric who drops a coin

in an open palm, the
calm virgin, and the child
on her lap, reaching out

to the world — the solid
flesh, round limbs and faces,
peaceful eyes. What burdens

there are — the crucified
God, somehow in repose,
or the crippled beggar

balanced on his crutch — are
made beautiful, an all–
too–human transgression,

a strange kindness, so that
the torment of the sick,
of the tortured martyrs,

their headless bodies that
once were bathed in pain, and

are now covered with the
light of grace, are simply

a matter of course, bright
red spatters of blood an

inevitable turn
of events, like the folds
of the red and green robes

of witnesses and of
victims alike. Rilke

must have been thinking of
him when he asked, whom can
we ever turn to in

our need — the light, at last,
a mystery to the
lost and to the redeemed.

Poem for Jackson Mac Low

Jackson Mac Low is no longer
among us, yet as luck would have
it, on my way up the street this
early March day, heading to his

memorial at St. Mark's Church,
I hear a sparrow, whose wants, of
all birds, have always seemed the most
simple — to nest unoffended,

to gather with its neighbors what
is needed for getting through the
dark time, whose chirp, a workaday,
ordinary sound, makes a lie

of the busy, complicated
life it leads after all — singing
in the bare branches and bright sun
an exquisitely intricate

spring song. I stop at a café
to sip a strong coffee, and through
the picture window take in the
light while Judy Collins's voice,

serendipity itself, as
delicate as "the sweetness of
the new time," fills the room. I can't
help thinking of his oddnesses,

mysteries of number and name,
how the line would play itself out,
and then the next, and then the next,
the moment about to happen.

Tuft of Lavender
Leeds, England 11.7.06

The tuft of Lavender
and little bees in the
sun, as if they were all —

how odd that somewhere there
might be another one,
the flowering of the

day, this sun, some other
place where we might sit for
a while, or never move.

Raking the Leaves

My father holds his rake beside him after
sweeping up the fallen, brittle leaves on this
chilly November day. The sun is strangely
bright for this time of year and we know the cold
is sure to come. He leans over, a little
out of breath, as if he were studying the
black asphalt of his driveway, and looks to be
answering a question he feels I will not
ask. "I'm not going to make it much longer,"
he says, without ceremony, and I, too,
stare down at the ground, and start to nod my head.

As long as I have lived, whatever he has
said to me, in the moment, of the facts of
our lives, has somehow embarrassed me, his way
of making things plain — as if, in my silence,
I had not thought of them — and of course his death,
not far off, is a secret I have chosen
to keep to myself. Riding home on the train,
thinking of my daughter, I resolve that when
I am old I will not speak of what will make
her sad, yet now, in the dark days of autumn,
I know what is possible and what is not.

That Boy
After lines by Michael Heller

"We are not ourselves
but the paradox,
we are no other."
Why is it that we
recall the oddest
things, years afterward,

when in the moment
we took no notice?
I stand before my

mirror, a graying
man I do not know —
instead, in my mind,
there is a boy with
a round face, dark eyes
and hair, shaping a

pompadour with his
hands, combing through it
over and over,

but it will not stay,
and so he tugs his
hair, finally, and
the tears in his eyes
are more now than I
can bear. I am that

boy, unable to
comb away the years
from in front of me,

peering on ahead
until, one day, they
are somehow gone, and
I can see how to
live there, in the past,
my eyes mine at last.

"Queen's View" of Loch Lomond*
10 August 2005

Rooftops of a village
and a stand of trees in
a valley, the heather

bellying down to the
water, Ben Lomond just

beyond as if we could
make our way there, old heart
worn down by wind, by rain —

time comes to those who walk
the hills in mist, in sun.

Here, today, we follow
the ancient path she loved,
earth heaved up long ago.

*A favorite trail of Queen Victoria

Plan

He leans across the table,
smiling as she speaks, listens
carefully to what she has
to say, and stirs his coffee,
leaving the spoon to stick out

of the cup before him. His
chin juts out at her. His eyes
watch her lips move. She sits up
tall when she talks and opens
her palms on either side of

her to make herself plain. She
explains her plan — what they will
do in the coming days, what
they have to buy for the new
apartment, what they do not

yet own, what will make sense, since
they will live together. It
is at this moment the food
arrives — the waiter, standing
over them patiently, a

plate in each hand, places the
morsels of their life between
them to seal their pact. They start
to eat, lost, for a moment,
in a sudden, new silence.

The Coming Snow

It's not so strange how
a day turns gray in
winter, without the
slightest hope of an

afternoon sun — long
since the bright, brief dawn.
Now is a time when
we can be sure of
a storm, the stark cold

suddenly come on
the wind. Indoors, we
sit, sipping coffee

and conversation —
no sense thinking of
the end of things, though,

how each of us will
slip into bed from
where, through a window,

one can witness the
graceful descent of
white, its delicate
curtain covering
the world in silence.

Ed Ruscha's *Course of Empire*
Whitney Museum, 19 November 2005

The clouds overhead,
dark filaments of
a roughed-up sky — the

wind from somewhere has
taken us all for
a wild ride — crossing

a frontier, the new
world coming all at
once upon us, and

below them, on the
side of the building's
plain façade the words
TOOL & DIE, as if

the made world were now
complete, what we had
wanted all along,

as if what has now
happened were something,
something we need not
think of again, for

the world can be made
again, a place where
everything is

in its place, the white
building, the simple
lettering stating
the facts, dark sky as

in a photograph
from some other time,
its shades of gray, and

glimmers of brightness
as well, but looking
up is for those who
love oblivion.

Susan Sontag Has Died

Time — over time
the body slips

away — nothing
is ever what

it is supposed
to be, illness

as metaphor.
As if without

fanfare, slowly,
in increments,

we lose the ones
we love. And we

lose ourselves. Death,
with the softest

of hellos, an
old friend we have

never met, drops
by one day for

a coffee and
conversation.

The body, the
body fails, at

last disappears
— yet we keep on

talking. A light
streams across the

table, its cups,
saucers and spoons,

these the remains
of a good life.

Seasonal

After the hard, steady rain, a dank day
in early November, we walk along
a path full of leaves — though the trees' branches

above us are not yet bare, the thin rays
of the afternoon sun, still enough red
and gold to comfort us, to keep us from
admitting the dark and cold into our

hearts. It is strange how, year after year, each
season slowly makes itself felt — one day,
the next, without our notice — until, all

at once, we are surprised at how we knew
the time would come, how the past is quite far
away. Yet today we still recall warmth

and light, even in this first chill, though now
I almost ache for the long darknesses
and the wild, unkempt winds in which my
griefs, grievances and grudges will find their

long sought home, even while we are homeless —
as we look toward the winter solstice, the
turn of the night, and then the startling spring.

Old Age Home

The ride from Manhattan — slipping her
into the passenger seat, swinging
in her legs, shutting the door — to the
suburbs of New Jersey, its trees and
freshly-painted houses, was as neat
as her empty apartment. We placed
some photos on her table, hung up
a few paintings on the walls, arranged
some of her sculptures here and there, plugged
in lamps and the television set.

We made our way along the hallway
to a room full of sun, where people
were gathered to talk a little, though
she had nothing to say. There was a
stereo playing music, and once
in a while someone sang the lyrics,
which had returned from some dim region —
a man seated in an easy chair
had wanted, years ago, "a girl just
like the girl who married dear old Dad."

We went to dinner. Someone poured her
a glass of juice. She ate, spilling food,
with a sudden hunger. Afterward
we sat on some couches. Someone asked
her to dance. The music played. She danced
with slight, tentative steps, a tulip
too heavy for its stem. When we had
to go we kissed goodnight, and left her
to lie down in her soft bed, her head
on her pillow, to slip into sleep.

Cicadas, July

The cicadas have arrived
with the morning patches of
sunlight caught in the leaves of
our backyard maple tree.

Everywhere their whirr fills the
the summer day with restlessness
and confuses the birds whose
signals have come to an end.

Unfolding from their pupae,
glistening for a moment,
these strangest of all creatures
tell us what heat is about.

They lie hidden in the grass,
though a bird's beak might pierce their
bravura, while we long for
the quiet and cool evening.

Richard Pousette-Dart's *Night Landscape*, 1969-71
Guggenheim Museum, New York City 8.22.07

The stars and other detritus
of the vast explosion of space
appear all at once and seek out
that secret, still spot within us,
and stir us there — so strange, unlike
anything we might ever know.

The night sky is a dream in which
we float free among the gaudy
lights, where there is no such thing as
darkness and what holds the stars there
are our hopes, like them pulsing and
signaling what we cannot read.

For every star crossing the deep
night, flaring and brilliant, someone
slips into sleep and dreams of a
lost star, a forgotten life quite
unlike what the daylight reveals
yet somehow very much the same.

Start of Day

In the small beauty of the forest
– George Oppen

The start of day in bright April,
the sun low across the grass and

in the shrubs and trees where there are
several birds of various

colors, hidden among the small,
new leaves — calling to each other

in their pitches and repeats, a
whirl and stutter, or a whistle

in a long loop — and then the red
flash of a cardinal flitting by

in the silence of its flight. I
think how, in spring's sudden beauty,

I am alive — as if drawing
a breath of air for the first time.

Crumbs upon the Table

We sit together
in the early light,
only half awake,

eating the first food
of the day, and let
some crumbs fall upon

the table, talking
about the terrors
in the morning news

on the radio —
and I think of how
beautiful you are,

and imagine what
you will do when you
leave for school, what peace

I will make with the
world, what bargain will
be struck. Casually,

you brush the crumbs to
the floor, turn your back,
pick up your coat and

bag, peer into the
mirror a moment,
and go out the door.

Two Blackbirds

The blackbird walks along the fence,
placing one foot, the other, on
each pinnacle, and standing still,
legs splayed, a claw wrapped around a
wooden spike, leans forward, peering
through the tree's leaves covering him
over, looks around, his partner,
on a nearby branch, doing the same.

Perhaps Starlight

Her skinny body is white as a harvest moon.
— Simon Pettet

You lean back from your plate
of carefully cut-up
food, small morsels arranged
just so, propped on the arm
of our sofa, a thin
hand and arm proffering
your fork in the air, your
legs extended as if
in a fashion photo —

maybe an issue of
a magazine on clothes
that flutter in the wind
when lying on white sand
beside green, tropical
waves. What could be lighter,
more ethereal, than
a summer breeze? Perhaps

starlight? Your beauty is
as delicate. That
we eat together is
not merely the will to
live, but an act of love.
I want to hold onto
what disappears, to the
empty moonlight, to the
starlight that barely glows.

Three Women Smoking Cigarettes

They sit at their tables
at the outdoor café,
their chairs turned to the side,
facing each other, their
cigarettes propped between
their long fingers, and they

talk. One of them laughs as
she nods her head. There
is something to what her
friend has said. The day moves
on. People on the street
pass them by. One of them

takes off her sunglasses
when a shadow from some
passing cloud covers them
over. I cannot see
her eyes from where I sit
on the other side of

the picture window, but
what she says, I know, is
important. Everything
is at stake. She lights the
next cigarette and it
is time, now, for me to

leave. I walk out the door
and pass them by through the
smoke that dissolves slowly
in the warm air. I hear
her say she will be back
tomorrow — as will I.

The Sleep of the Dead

My mother would sleep "the sleep of the dead,"
she used to say. We would wake her and she
would sigh, saying she had slept longer than
she had meant to. On the day my father
was to leave our home he lay in bed with
his back to her, a single tear in his
eye — and she, breathing softly, lay with her
back to him. "I wake to sleep," Roethke wrote.
In her sleep she seemed to leave her daily
torments behind with her two sons, boyfriends,
job, landlord, books, music, movies, paintings
and sculptures — as if sleep were without thought,
without language or dream, the stepping out
of time and into a still and deep lake.

In her old age she grew sick, too full of
pain to walk more than a few steps from her
bed. One night, after a light meal with wine,
she fell asleep. When we found her in the
morning she was lying on her side, her
arm crooked at the elbow and tucked under
her pillow, her eyes and lips closed, her cheek
smooth. A thin thread of saliva and blood
had trickled from the corner of her mouth
and turned brittle on her chin. Her heart had
surged and stopped. She looked like she had not known
it. Perhaps that night she dreamed — dreaming of
lying in her mother's arms, of sinking
into the calm water of her embrace.

Home from the War

They sit upright, talking
quietly. One of them

has his arm stretched out to
hold onto a cup of

coffee. Their faces are
newly shaven and their

heads are bare except for
a short tuft of hair on

top. Their smooth, muscular
arms and necks emerge out

of their tight t-shirts. A
pretty young woman sets

down some plates of food in
front of them — a sandwich,

salad, and a bowl of
soup for her, as she seats

herself in between their
wheelchairs and swings her legs

underneath the table,
taking up her napkin

and spoon. Whose girlfriend is
she, which one of them, with

his buddy, home now from
the war? Spring sunlight pours

through a nearby window,
suddenly covering

their faces — this lazy
Saturday afternoon.

Washing My Brother's Hair

He leans forward on his knees,
offering himself to me
to wash, turned around to the
foot of his hospital bed.

I think there is much to say,
since he has come here to die
and I have come for one last
visit — this time together.

But what there is to be done
is really quite simple, to
do for him what he cannot —
what comfort there still might be.

I set up a basin of
warm water and wet his head,
and anoint it with shampoo,
my hands swirling in his hair.

My fingers rub his scalp and
feel the odd bumps and hollows
of the skull his hair hides as
if they were embarrassments.

He seems like that helpless child
who crawled into my bed at
night, afraid of the dark — two
young boys left alone and frail.

Some days later, when I kiss
his cold forehead and hold his
stiff body to me, I think
of the man he had become.

Late February Snow

Late February snow has fallen
in the night, and I no longer
remember what it was I wanted,

stepping into the morning sun,
the spring not so far off after all.
I give myself over to the

day, a reluctant lover who can
forget and be content. The light
fills the expanse of white, the cold in

my clothes, and I am walking with
no place special to go, and I think
how this just might last forever.

Café in Maplewood

He sits tall in his highchair, arms above
his head, kicking his feet, smiling at us
as we pass him. A waiter stops clearing
a nearby, abandoned table of its
dishes and cups to wave hello, calling
him away from the spoonful of food his
mother proffers and the napkin in his
father's hand meant to wipe his mouth — and when
he laughs we all laugh with him, as if the
day has turned out to be a grand success
although it is just past noon. And I guess
it has, the room filled with people at lunch.

We hover about our young. We welcome
them into their world, as wonderful or
terrible as it can be. Even those
who outlived the camps (on their arms those blue,
simple numbers) would smile at me as they
turned away from their conversation, a
boy seated in the warm kitchen of his
grandmother, where above the stove on the
wall a framed doily read, "If contentment
is the theme, life's melody is sweet." She
had set out from Russia, a girl alone.

She landed at Ellis Island and made
her way to Chicago and then returned
to New York with a sick husband and four
children, to the shtetl of Brownsville
in Brooklyn, to Herzl Street named for the great
Zionist. So her dream and destiny
became this neighborhood of people–filled streets,
three shuls on her block, gangsters among
them from Murder, Inc. Now here I am in
a café in Maplewood, New Jersey,
full of hope, trying to write this poem.

Summer's End

A squawk in the
bushes then a
red flitting from

branch to branch, the
cardinal in
the cool sun, days

ago the light
bright and hot, now
no doubt what will

come — a squirrel
skitters along
the fence and leaps

into a tree.

Edvard Munch's *Despair*, 1892
Museum of Modern Art, New York City 2006

He is looking over the rail
of the promenade, but he sees
nothing, caught in the thought of the
helpless — no, not even a thought —

despair itself, as undefined
as the dark, thick brushstrokes, the stabs
of green paint below his blank face.
People walk and talk together,

out of earshot, making plans, while
the red sky, its long cloudless arcs,
surges above blue hills hugging
the sea, its ships making their way.

Friends Gone

The late autumn sunlight settles
among the scattered leaves, squirrels,
and birds, in the cool air after
yesterday's rain — strange populous

backyard, all creatures suddenly
busy making preparations,
not simply waiting for the snow
and the deep, long darkness to come.

I fill the bird feeder with seed
and rake the leaves — the long winter
soon to arrive at our doorstep —
now, each year, recalling friends

gone forever, more gone than here,
it seems, yet the landscape no more
bare, and the sun, for a while still,
shedding its thin remnants of warmth.

Brighton Beach, August

White sails cutting through dark blue water
in a bright, hot light — crisscrossing the
odd speedboat, freighter, barge and tugboat
set on a sure course — they turn their sharp
pirouettes, one with another, as
if ocean birds with their wide wings who
pivot, dive, soar, and glide across the
big sky, or paper kites high above
the beach, swirling on warm air currents.

We bury our feet along with the
poles of orange and green umbrellas,
staked in between oiled and tanned bodies
lying perfectly still, in the smooth
sand stretching away from the boardwalk's
hot wooden planks. Everything seems to
be floating off from solid earth in
the midday August delirium,
a fantasy without any end.

I think of the white cornettes Breton
women used to wear in another
time (in Basil King's painting after
Gaugin) — perhaps fashioned from sails or
gulls' wings — who might have spent a day by
the sea in Brest, having thrown off their
clothes to leap in the spray of the surf,
or, buoyed by the cool salt water,
to linger beyond the rolling waves.

From where we stand we listen to the
shore's immense quiet settling into
the afternoon along with the heat,
a child's playful scream dissolving in
the air all at once, and nearby the
loud arguments of old men playing
dominoes, smacking down their white tiles
on stone tables. Yet the sails are what
make it all come true, catching the breeze.

Gust of Winter Wind

The wind in the trees, as
if their branches would be
torn away from their trunks
and blown over rooftops —

we stand below, squinting
into the thin daylight,
the birds, the squirrels gone,
bare hours all there are.

Getting Old

The meal is done, and so they
dig in their bags for money
to pay the check, and gather

up their coats but stand by their
table, talking, the dishes
and cups no longer arranged

for their entrance — the grandness
of it all. They cannot leave,
slightly hunched over before

each other. There is much to
say. And at the next table
he sits alone, over a

coffee, reading the sports page
of today's newspaper spread
from hand to hand, his head tipped

forward and the slight pull of
his lips at the corners of
his mouth, a smile at the scores

of pre-season baseball games,
the earned runs, errors, stolen
bases. We are all of us

here. Spring will be coming soon.
That we know this to be has
become important, just as

is the afternoon light. He
at his table, they at theirs,
we will stay here forever.

Abandoned House

Thin tendrils of moss,
bright green in the shock
of morning sun across
red brick steps, stand up
straight to touch the light.

After Robert Creeley

> *what*
>
> *can I say to*
> *you — words, words*
> *as if all*
> *worlds were there.*
>   — Robert Creeley

The embrace
is all there
is — what can

be said, all
the things of
this world, are

left behind,
abandoned.
And yet there

are words, words,
which we love.
You wrote a

poem for
the doctor,
your father

poet, whose
name was not
the point, yet

there were words
between you.
You praised the

smallest of
them. Even
and became

just so. These
things are what
we hold to

us. Then let
us embrace
them — because

we would hold
each other.
The body,

the body
can give way
to our words —

to which we
must cling. The
things of this

world, let us
celebrate
the littlest

of them — *the*,
by, *upon*,
you, *me*, *us*.

Birdfeeder

Don't you know that lovers
like to imagine eternity

while a sparrow pecks at candy wrappers
— D. Nurske

Frenzy of fluttering wings, the flock
of sparrows floats near the birdfeeder,

two or three at a time alighting
as best they can on the small perches,

poking their beaks through the apertures,
seeking the sweet food in the see-through

cylinder (amber, yellow, mixed with
the odd black seeds of wildflowers) —

the whole apparatus, its cluster
of birds, swaying slowly below the

eave of the tool shed — summer's end,
what is left in memory. It has

become the business of all creatures
to search for sustenance where they might

— I among them, in the morning light,
though sitting apart at my table,

reading the newspaper, who, like them,
knows the coming evening will arrive

suddenly and the cold quite soon. The
birds gather tentatively — until,

all at once, with a flurry, they fly
off in a sure knot. The squirrel close

by claws up the maple tree beside
me — which still casts some shade — up to its

highest branch, posing there, ready to
leap. Below, the cat from next door makes

her steady way from behind a bush
and onto the newly trimmed grass — her

careful prancing a pure grace. We all
want to live, but I alone will mourn

the relentless passing of the days.

The Sapling

The sapling, smooth
bark and a few
thin branches, points
upward toward the
sun while its roots
seek sustenance
deep underground —
the search for light,
for water — so
that after a
great many years

a tree will fill
the sky, and on
this spring morning
there is something
softer than wood,
slightly green, at
the tip of a
branch, a first bud,
a leaf to come,
to tremble in
a summer breeze.

Big Wind in a Small Town

Sun and a big wind
fill the small street, the

broad and bright banners
waving and flapping,

breaking loose from their
tethers, muffling the

hum of cars rolling
slowly by, telling

of the new drama
set to take place in

the little theatre
at the far end of

town, and children run
beside their strollers

along the sidewalk,
their mothers yelling

to be careful, and
in the sudden, sharp

cold the sparrows tuck
their heads down, deep and

low in the bushes,
as the leaves in the

trees above are stripped
away, and shoppers

with their bags of food
step on and off the

curbs. Surely there is
something about to

happen, but we are
all on our ways off

to somewhere, no time
to stop, take notice

— except for the birds,
those who have remained,

no long flight to sweet
southern realms, a far

branch to wait out the
longer nights to come.

Start of Spring

Stems set in the clear glass vase,
standing straight in their water,
the sun through the window — and,
no doubt, the songs of birds, small
creatures, beyond the front door —
these red tulips bend toward this
early morning's bright spring light.

Hameau de l'Eglise 8.25.05
Notre Dame de Bliquetuit, Normandy

Garden café,
a stone wall and
church beyond, we
sip coffee and

wonder how long
the light will last,
the sun's hard warmth.
Late August, the

frost sure to come
one night, just as
the small triumphs
of the day, and

no matter what
the tower's bells
ring at noon, it
seems, forever —

the call to be
born and to pass
from us, to be
remembered. The

kindness of late
summer — no sure
sign of winter's
darkness and cold —

the pigeons coo
until the purr
of an engine
on the distant

road overtakes
us all, until
we slip into
the great unknown.

Early March Afternoon

The mother, father and grown
daughter sit in overcoats,
bending over their soup and

bread, and look out the window
in silence at winter's end —
its raw insistence, the bite

of its wind, its bitter dark —
but now the bright, blinding sun
fills the room for a moment.

The Seeds of the Red Maple

Overnight the red maple in our backyard,
provider of shade when leaves are full and days
are hot, and of majesty even when bare
in winter, has let go of its seeds, now at
mid summer, in the joy of light and
grief of time taking its inevitable
shape, the season giving in to its own pulse,
the maple's colors soon to turn once again.

The tree's fruit keys* are everywhere, in grass and
shrubs and covering the patio flagstones
and table at which I write this poem, their
strange green casings joined to one another as
if in an eternal kiss, their oddly shaped
wings, whose reticulate filaments emerge
out of a leathery spine, mimicking the
half moon, its glow doing the dark's secret work.

Children, splitting the husks open to find the
sticky pith within (which squirrels love to eat
raised up on haunches, forepaws in a flurry,
their frantic chewing the hint of an autumn
recklessness when winter food must be stored), fix
the wings to their noses so they are marked as
people of the tree, yet other seeds will fly
free, taking their tenacious hold in the soil.

---

*A *fruit key* or simply *key* or *samara* is a type of seed or pod of seeds in which a flattened wing of fibrous, papery tissue, called a *wing*, develops from the ovary wall.

Lido Cristoforo Columbo
8.16.05

Rome is the city of bells
and fountains whose water has

run down from the seven hills,
and cars, trolleys, buses that

mark the stands of palm and pine,
cutting off pedestrians,

crossing each other's path — and
trains taking everyone to

some other destination.
Rome is the city of popes,

but today we prefer the
sun and summer breezes of

the beach. So we hop on the
lido transit leaving on

the half hour, making its way
inexorably to the sea

where the wind carries the cries
of children who stumble out

of the waves as if they have
lost their way in the heat. We

lie still in the bright light and
somehow remember the bells.

The Cardinal

Red flash and quick chirp
from a branch of the
backyard maple tree

reaching across the
neighbor's fence, casting
a shade in sunlight —

the cardinal flies
free, flits among leaves,
suddenly drops down

into the tall grass,
jerks his head this way
and that, hops and turns,

then leaps up into
the green above, no
longer to be seen.

Variation of Green
Ellsworth Kelly at the Met 3.16.06

The idea of green. That there are verities.
– William Bronk

A new, bright sun, the first of
spring's signals in a brisk breeze,

might make us think of the grand
landscape whose wind in the trees

startles mythical creatures
awake, the hills, the sweep of

a cloudy, furious sky.
Yet there is a purer form,

a sure possibility,
the simple color, at once

dependable and filled with
our dearest ghosts, whose fable

of the unknown beckons — the
shock of red or gradations

of green in which the world, a
world beyond green, has never

been known — for what is there to
know? What is there is just there,

and we stand alongside it
in astonishment, taking

shelter in its glow, against
the insistence of winter.

Visiting the Nursing Home

Too weak for talk, she
looks up at me and
blinks her eyes, while I
settle her into
a wheelchair and roll
it through the door — out

into the spring sun
where, hidden among
the new leaves on the
distant trees, birds are
singing. I lift her
onto a white wood

bench, and she leans back,
closes her eyes and
lets the light cover
her face. Heading home,
I stop for a while
at a café where

a mournful trombone
solo is filling
the room, and then a
piano starts up —
in its counterpoint
I imagine the

pianist's nimble
fingers as they run
over the blank keys,
then pausing to hold
down a chord, and then
another, the horn's

supple riffs caught in
between. There are things
we must do while we
can, like make music
or this sad poem —
what is possible.

Laocoön and His Sons, Museo Vaticani
12 August 2005

The ancient Greeks knew the way
of muscle, the way of bone,
the torque of desire, the

look of pain, of yearning for
release, the ecstasy of

sinuous bodies as they
enfold one another and

the cold animal thrown up
from the sea — how tightly it
winds itself about them — the

agony of belief and
their shock of recognition

in the serpent's grasp. Standing
before my mirror, I run

my hands over my shoulders
and chest, the musculature

of an aging man thinking
about athletic love but
also your simple touch, your

hand. What swirling flesh would then
enfold me? We will lie down

together, having made a
peace with the world, its lost time.

"I Feel a Song Comin' On"
After viewing *Let's Get Lost*

When Chet Baker sings, the wind waves
the trees' branches as if, with their
caresses, they soften the fears
of creatures, and in his wince of
ecstasy, as he holds a note

longer than he should, the evening
breeze can be forgiven for its
gentle ministrations of the
lost souls who will never keep their
word. And when he picks up his horn

and plays, the rivers overflow
their banks and flood the fields, and the
sea off Malibu runs up the
beach and carries it away, a
thief in the night. And by the time

Chet Baker's song is through a mist
has settled on a dark road and
a hitchhiker walking into
the hills beyond. No wonder that
women loved him, even when he

left them to their children, and dope
pushers knocked out his front teeth. The
truth is that music can make the
weather and make us all crazy,
even now that he is long gone.

Neighbors

Under the backyard maple tree
we sip our morning tea and read
the Sunday paper, the summer
sun already above branches
whose shade crosses our table full
of cups, spoons, teapot, and napkins.

In the bushes beyond, sparrows
chirp at a robin who has flown
too close to their nest, and somewhere
not far away a knife and fork
scrape a plate of the day's first food.

The Deception
Still Life by Giorgio Morandi, 1955
New York Metropolitan Museum of Art, 2008

How easily we settle
into the picture — four plain
boxes and a single long–
necked bottle — simple objects
arranged together so he
might catch them in their soft browns
and yellows, and among them
an intransigent, opaque
white spot, but everywhere else
in the canvas black traces
he must have applied with the
most informal of brush strokes.

He means to discomfort us
yet we surrender ourselves
to these sure shapes assembled
as for a camera, though
without occasion, nothing
to be done, since it is best,
he must have thought, once he knew
he loved to paint, to leave things
unspoken — the mute smears of
color, the bare ground of the
horizontal — a made world,
his stubborn craft what there is.

House, Normandy
21 August 2005

The bee bends to
the thistle. The
chestnut tree lets

go of its fruit.
We cling to the
late summer light.

The hedge around
the house has grown
wild, but the gate

is open to
show we are home.
Stone walls have stood

these four hundred
years — since someone,
much like us, first

thought about the
sun, rain and wind.
This bright morning

we sit and sip
our coffee, the
dew everywhere,

moss on the bricks
beneath our feet.
The day will come,

perhaps, when the
the forest will
enfold us all.

Even the stones
will disappear,
left abandoned.

Snow Shine

Late winter's frozen
ground, and through the bare
branches of the trees

the new sun shines its
light on the hard white
snow for the sake of
the days to come, and

a bird stabs at the
great silence broken
by the crack of ice
from far off — the same
note four, five times, then

a pause — the sparest
of offerings, and
before long a most
tentative, fragile

desire takes shape, the
green tendril pushing
through, and spring's bright trill.

Bar Mitzvah

They stand before the ark — rabbi,
cantor, the boy between them, draped
in white prayer shawls, heads covered by
embroidered skull caps — and draw back
the curtains to reveal the scrolls

covered in their opulent sheath
of bejeweled dark felt cloth, red
and blue stones held in place as if
by a deep night. While the one sings
the other, a tall man, reaches
in and lifts the hidden text, the
sacred law, onto his shoulder,

and they come among us, we who
touch the living Torah with our
books of prayer or silken tassels
and then touch our lips to seal our
pact with the invisible God.

The three of them return to where
they began, and the boy, looking
into the rabbi's eyes, takes the
scripture from his arms and staggers
for a brief moment under the
heavy weight, steadying himself,
while this man removes its cover,

and then together they settle
it on the podium so it
might be unrolled to the proper
spot, as the cantor ends his prayer.
The rabbi takes up the silver

cursor and directs the boy to
where he must begin, and so the
boy intones his bare entreaties
until the moment when the small
children run up behind him to
shower him with bags of candy.
At this instant he is a man.

On Raccoon Ridge
Near the Delaware Water Gap, 10.25.08

The pensive man . . . He sees the eagle float
For which the intricate Alps are a single nest.
— Wallace Stevens

A mile's climb up, crossing slabs of old rock
and fallen trees sunken in soil over
time, stair steps where we place our feet, out of
breath at the top, all of a sudden the
wide sky and beyond the valley a red,
orange and yellow canopy, Diane
and I pass a canteen of water back
and forth, then move on along the ridge in
the open air and great silence until
we find a large boulder, half buried, then
sit there to look out on the bright day, and
dig into our backpacks for sandwiches
we eat slowly, savoring our good luck.

In a close-by sapling the smallest bird
we have ever seen, what looks to be an
insect, flits from one branch to the next, its
tan feathers not unlike the leaves, while a
black hawk, wings extended, floats on an air
current below us, scanning the distant
ground for the quick tremor of a bush or
the parting of grass where a rabbit or
squirrel has lost sight of the sky, but, no
sign of food, the hunter lets a breeze lift
it through the gulf, the late afternoon sun
at its back, and from the tree near us the
tiny animal flies into the woods.

Tilted Arc
After the Richard Serra Retrospective
Museum of Modern Art, New York City, 8.11.07

I run my hand across
your shoulders and along
your spine that dips and then
rises, and I am in
no hurry — for once there
is nowhere I need to go.

There is the curve of space
people speak of and there
are the soft curves of your
body, and I suppose
his arc tells us of this —
of how we move with ease.

We walk, dance, lie down and
curl ourselves up to sleep.
We obey the pull of
the earth, moon, sun, stars and
perhaps the emptiness
of space an arc holds still.

It seems as if we might
sight its trajectory
off to the horizon
and never arrive home —
never grow old, sailors
on an endless voyage.

Yes, the shaped steel changes
color in the rain, light,
and wind as months, years
pass by, softens somehow
before our eyes, under
the touch of fingertips.

Yet there is that which we
will never get used to.
We might sway in time with
the turning planet, while
the arc tilts above us,
casting its strange shadow.

The Waves

When you told me, "I'm dying — it's
all right," I dreamt I was treading
water in the ocean, no land

in sight, and a great ship, its sails
jutting into the night sky, was

making its slow way toward the far
horizon. The world of the dead
must be like that realm where dreams hold

the living, where we come and go,
breathing stars. If I could rouse you

from that place I would tell you how
I swam, swam to shore, exhausted,
where I hear your voice in the waves.

Monet's Garden
Giverny, 20 August 2005

The lily's charm is not
its colors but how it
floats, as if free, upon

the pond's dark surface. We
make our way over his

wooden bridge and then pass
the shrubs and flowers he
planted, arranged just so

to paint. How carefully
the pigment would be placed,

how gradually the world —
its daily businesses —
would become still and deep.

Jane Planting Flowers
Spring 2010

She tilts her head to view
the white impatiens she
holds in her hand, the light
of the afternoon caught
in them — thinking where they

belong among blue and
yellow petals on their
stems newly rooted in
black loam. She has come home
as if to arrange our

garden this spring — having
left her stray–dog artist's
life in the city for
a time, its car alarms,
gritty sidewalks and shared

apartments. I say how
lovely the backyard looks
and will not let on her
sitting there, at the edge
of the grass, is what I

mean — this sunny day in
the shade of our maple
tree from which she used to
swing, years ago, until
it was too dark to see.

Marlene Dumas' *The Kiss*, 2003
Museum of Modern Art, New York City, 2009

What might not be dreamt
in the stupor of
Saturday night by
herself — she lies face
down against the white

sheets on her bed, the
dark line of her sealed
eyelids, her lips just
barely apart that
had once said his name.

Late January Morning

I step out the door on this
somber, cold January
morning to get the daily
newspaper tossed onto my
lawn covered snow white though it
is still before dawn, and as

I bend down I hear a bird
on a distant bare branch of
a tree singing a song I
have last heard when there were leaves
everywhere I looked — a call
to meet, to feather the nest —

so what could it mean in these
dark days? Perhaps, as I have
done, simply contemplating
a moment in my modest
domestic life, this bird has
foolishly, proudly proclaimed

it has a home — no need to
fly south — against the stark chill,
tempting the fates, and knowing,
more than I who will migrate
to my kitchen for some tea,
the nights are getting shorter.

Alhambra Steps

Leaving the palace
we descend the steep
stone stairs arm in arm —
you pulling me down,
me holding you up.

Mikvah,* Warsaw Ghetto 1941
At a screening of *A Film Unfinished*, New York City 2010

They wade into the
water, naked, in
silence, shoulders hunched
over, in their fear
betraying the lens.

There are dark splotches
in the celluloid
where their groins were and
where the soldiers, out
of the frame, could aim.

In far off Berlin
an information
officer realized
what he was seeing,
hid it in a vault.

A young girl in the
ghetto who by luck
has become an old
woman, is being
shown the restored film.

Watching the haggard
bodies, the clumsy
attempts to obey,
she sighs as if she
has to be polite.

"When the Germans showed
up there was always
trouble," she says, the
fact of the matter
unalterable.

*A Jewish ritual bath used for immersion in a purification ceremony.

Big Storm

Beneath the eave
the birdfeeder
swinging in swirls
of driven snow —

bluejays, sparrows
and cardinals
gather as if
a single flock

in the white air
flying to the
hoard of seeds, its
scarce sustenance —

blue, brown and red
birds daring each
other for a
tenuous perch.

With Fred Caruso, Standing in Front of Pierre Bonnard's
Corner of the Dining Room at Le Cannet
"The Late Interiors," Metropolitan Museum of Art,
New York City, 27 March 2009

Nothing much ever happens, yet there
is a comfort in simply living
among the objects of the day — bowls
of fruit, a vase of flowers on a
red tablecloth holding light coming
from a window outside of the frame.

Her face is turned sideways above her
bright yellow shawl as she looks for what
she has meant to take with her, leaving
the room — or is she, in a backward
glance at the urn on the mantelpiece,
admiring her arrangements of things?

Fred and I stand talking, the painting
of the dining room behind him, and
I think about Bonnard's soft tones, then
about Fred's portrayals in their hot
colors, his people — young and full with
desire, and smiling at the viewer.

In Bonnard's picture we slowly come
to notice a faint longing in the
day itself — the woman's dissolving
thought, what she wants still remaining, like
the scene before us, which is not quite
real but true enough for the moment.

On a Terrace, Waiting to Enter *El Palacio Nazaríes, Alhambra*

A man reads
of the old
palace out
loud from his
French brochure.

His wife stares
across the
valley to
the mountains
in their snow.

Cicadas, Mid July

How odd the occasion, the whirring
of the cicadas, surprising once
we start to hear their secret business,
unseen no matter where we look — we
pause in our morning talk, wondering
when they arrived and why the summer's
unforgiving heat begins with their
advent and later the cool early
evenings settle in with their silence.

In its false starts with the pushing through
soil and snow of its first flowers, their
small shocks of color, spring held us
in blossoms and leaves — so we finally
let go of the thought that the light and
warmth would ever come to an end, but
the cicadas do their work, no more
twitters of birds, our sadness spun in
the din and the waning of the light.

Stone Love
Metropolitan Museum of Art, New York City, 15 May 2011

for Jayne Holsinger and Hugh Seidman

The round torsos
hide the stone for
a moment, the
idea there

of bodies pressed
together, their
resilient flesh
in form itself.

Later I walk
down the street and
young couples pass
me arm in arm,

lost in spring's warmth
— the fact of love,
how we believe
in it, its touch.

Summer, Young Woman by the Westside Drive

She walks along the
river, one hand to
her ear, talking on
her telephone in
the afternoon sun.

The cars and trucks on
the drive pass her by,
speeding the other
way, their small breezes
easing the vast heat.

She trails her other
hand behind, fingers
brushing the hedge tops
planted beside the
way, their dried spring buds.

Her black dress, swirling
with each step, her bare
brown shoulders, arms and
legs gather in the
unforgiving light.

The Way We Live

The hole dug, a few words spoken, we
are invited to cast the unearthed
soil upon the coffin below,
its skillfully carved six-pointed star.

His two sons from among us take up
the shovel in turn, and then his wife,
sobbing, and the rest of us, stepping
to the edge, back to the gathering.

Someone remembers the ritual
flag but it is too late to drape it
over him, the younger son saying,
helpfully, "it will be a keepsake."

The rabbi in English rehearses
this man's life, his generosity
and laughter, how resourceful he was,
the good husband and father he was.

Named *Pesach*,* which became Paul, he spent
his first Passover away from home
on a troop ship in the Pacific,
about to land on Guadalcanal.

The rabbi tells us of the unique
kindness we perform in attending
a funeral, a *mitzvah*** the dead
do not know, which they cannot repay.

At last the sons intone the *Kaddish*,***
the older, his voice broken, convulsed
in sorrow, the Hebrew he studied
long ago alive for the first time.

---

*Hebrew and Yiddish for *Passover*.
**A good deed.
***Jewish prayer used to mourn the death of a close relative.

Wild Onions (After Robert's Letter)

For Robert and Elizabeth Murphy

I think if I were very old I
would want the wild onions growing in
my yard to take up housekeeping with
me — "their flower heads," once "bobbing
in the wind," poking from a jar as
they fade to a fine dust, so I might
see in them who I have become — more
lovely than I am in the morning
mirror where I glimpse who I once was.

Robin, Spring

The robin, claws hidden in
tall grass, hops forward and sings
a solitary note, hops
once more, stopping to sing two
notes, which loop through the air, then
tilts its head to eye the ground,
flies off to a nearby tree.

Late November in the South Mountain Reservation

The day has taken on a plan
in the brief warmth of a late fall
sun, so Diane and I start our
walk through the bare trees, having left
the car in a drift of wet red
leaves by the road — no deer, no bird
either, but the stone bridge ahead,
and beyond it the waterfalls.

We climb alongside the cold spray
to reach the stream above, soft spot
of the mountain where it might yield
to us — where we sit and pour tea
from a thermos, sipping it out
of paper cups, and I think of
the *chanoyu* ceremony*
as we watch the light on wet rocks.

---

*Japanese tea ceremony otherwise known as the Way of Tea, which involves the ritual preparation and presentation of particularly green tea.

Domestic

Cutting board, knife, bread
crumbs in the dawn light —
eating standing up
by the kitchen sink —
she went back to bed.

At a Willem de Kooning Show with Michael Heller
Pace Gallery on Fifty-Seventh Street, New York City, May 2011

Not a declaration which is truth
But a thing
Which is. It is the business of the poet
"To suffer the things of the world
And to speak them and himself out."
  – George Oppen

Broad swirling brush strokes crossing
the canvas, their edges fade
in thinned-out paint, and Mike talks
about how the bright yellow
leaks out of the light blue laid
on slightly thicker while I,
from over his shoulder, try

seeing what he sees — twisted
figures the colors make most
of all, what the artist saw
as his quandary, since what else
might have been the point? We drop
back onto the street and look
into the drizzle before

stepping on, the wild spring
among tall buildings that sound
the buses, trucks, taxicabs
bellying along the wet
swath of dark asphalt in their
commerce — not unlike, really,
"the business of the poet."

Storm, Beach, Gull
Belmar, New Jersey, August 2009

Spatters of rain in the wind hurrying us
along the boardwalk, its evenly laid planks
of wood, unlike the wild day, repeating
themselves on toward a low-lying roof in
the gray distance, the slate water covers and
uncovers the darkened beach where birds leap up
and settle again, picking at what they can.

A white gull tries to tear apart the neck and
breast of a small dead bird found in the sand, the
limp body flopping about in its great beak,
but then lets go and rises in the air,
heavy wings fully spread in the droplets of
storm, slowly flapping, the mute ocean
gathering up the carcass in its embrace.

Looking through the Picture Window at Poets House
Late March 2011, New York City

The filigree of twigs on bare
branches though the park, the river
beyond invisible in fog,
a woman pushes her baby
carriage along the street, holding
the hand of her older child,
a girl in red jacket and cap
prancing behind, looking away.

Early April Morning

dazed spring approaches
— William Carlos Williams

A few birds twirling their notes in
the new light and my neighbor, hunched
over his garden, the hood of
his sweatshirt keeping his thoughts
to himself, looks past me as I bend
to take hold of the newspaper
tossed on my walk before dawn when
wet, dense darkness was all there was —

but then I hear his "good morning,"
he and I standing upright for
a moment before his turn back
to work, the bamboo prongs of his
rake softly scraping the soil
the night's rain has softened, to make
ready for planting flowers, the
early hour otherwise still.

Arctic Terns

> *White clouds like kerchiefs at parting*
> *Are waved by the wandering wind,*
> *And the heart of the wind*
> *Aches at the silence of love.*
> — Pablo Neruda

Arctic terns touch down from the sky
every few years, leaving their life
of flight to raise their young and then,
in the waning light, lift off the
firm earth of Greenland to make their

way south — roving high above the
ocean, not too close to land but
looping east to trace the coast of
Africa or west along the
shores of South America, then

finally crossing the open
sea to the farthest reach of ice —
for a second season of days.
In large flocks they eye the water
for food, and once a male has fed

his future mate her fill of fish —
in a rite beyond gravity —
they join for their entire lives.
Yet flying must be an act of
solitude, an unfed longing.

Praise for Burt Kimmelman

"A rare evocation . . . the wonder of this world in itself."
— Robert Creeley

"Artful, fastidious, learned . . . I am delighted by so much feeling for style."
— Alfred Kazin

"The sense of number in his writing . . . the *littlest words* & the small moments through which we live . . . are of a piece. In this there is . . . a strict & powerful accounting, leaving me — for one — filled with admiration & hooked on every word."
— Jerome Rothenberg

"Few contemporary poets so gracefully demonstrate classic notions of what the practice of poetry must be: Kimmelman's work is carefully wrought, with concision, focus, and the rhythm of musical composition. . . . ."
— Madeline Tiger, *Jacket*

"In Burt Kimmelman's poems . . . form calls deeply to form, as though the works . . . lifted one to the very brim of language where one could speak . . . of a life caught whole."
— Michael Heller

"[In Kimmelman's poetry] the arts restate the questions we have been asking and the ways they clean and stretch our questions reward us more than answers would."
— William Bronk

"Kimmelman is a poet who obviously admires the clarity of classical Chinese poetry and strives for it in his tight syllabics and in his shifting images of light and dark. In doing so, he finds what is luminously transcendent in the routines of everyday life."
— Harvey Shapiro

"As quiet an experience as anyone could wish for."
— Cid Corman

"[Kimmelman's] poems evince a quality infrequently encountered in contemporary American poetry: modesty, an attentive and forthright modesty. . . . Modesty in an age of irony is infrequent, rare . . . worth our own best attention. These poems are 'worth it'."
— John Taggart

"Kimmelman's quiet poems contain the luminescence of perception, its lure, its beauty, its Zen of breath, tracing beauty in the pulse of the extant."
— Star Black

"Burt Kimmelman's sense of the whole poem, or what Zukofsky famously calls the "rested totality," is as impressive as that of his precursors [Oppen, Bronk, Creeley et al.], and in one respect, it exceeds them. He is a remarkably confident poet, though not confident in his self, his ego, or even his craft, his way with words, though he has every right to be. His confidence lies with the poem itself, that he has found it (or that it has found him), and that he can proceed through the poem, knowing that if he follows himself sincerely, the words will be there for him."
— Norman Finkelstein, *The Offending Adam*

"Exceptionally intelligent and necessary."
— Ed Foster, *The Poetry Project Newsletter*

"A verse so delicate and so far from insistence. . . . He seems to me at the beginning of 2012 the poet who takes the place of Rexroth, Blackburn, and Olson as a clean, clear, accessible starting point for any serious poet."
— Karl Young, *Light & Dust*

"Burt Kimmelman is a master of a poetry of cinematique. . . . [The] sense of place itself becomes a part of the theme of the work that it exists in . . . a world the very sights of which create a desire to understand its meaning and a need to accept what's seen as the stuff author and audience are made of."
— Sherry Kearns, *Home Planet News*

"Attains 'the simple . . . facts'."
— Samuel Menashe

"Burt Kimmelman sees with unerring clarity the small moments that enrich our lives. He doesn't pass through life blindly. He doesn't rage wildly. He searches for and celebrates each stark, harsh, sad, tender, and joyful moment through words and shares them freely."
— Laurel Johnson, *Midwest Book Review*

"Burt Kimmelman's poems flourish as they pivot from a repertoire of reiterated subjects — works of art, natural landscapes, family, the animal world — to a transfiguring notion of their properties and possibilities. [T]his practice has produced dynamic patterns of insight, patterns comprised of recurring figures and forms which nevertheless shift in their relations to his poetic witness."
— Jon Curley, *Talisman: A Journal of Contemporary Poetry and Poetics*

"[Kimmelman's work] coheres as tenderly as softly falling rain."
— Basil King

"Everything comes together so beautifully you will just feel sad it's ended. . . ."
— Kevin Killian, *Amazon Reviews*

"Kimmelman focuses on daily experiences in ways that make us take another look at them. He steps back to ponder, and in so doing, makes us do the same."
— William Allegrezza, *Galatea Resurrects*

"Finely tuned to the mute moments. . . ."
— James L. Weil

"The poems flex with perception and feeling."
— Bernie Earley, *Otoliths*

"The poems . . . have the spiritual resonance of a talented poet humble before nature, love, and language. In engaging a world larger than himself, Burt Kimmelman offers us poems that feel like a gift."
— Deborah Diemont, *New Pages*

"Precious is the chance to see what is unfolding before him, all that he is at the edge of."
— Kip Zegers, *Connotation Press Book Reviews*

"[Kimmelman's] poems capture details of life in quietly lyric ways as seemingly ephemeral as the moment they record. But they're deceptively so."
— Michael Lally, *Lally's Alley*

"The event is the silence of the moment."
— Corinne Robins

"We've waited some time to read something this intelligent, this sensuous and this crystalline. In fact, *Somehow* calls out with our words to make phrases, to mythologize our existence, to speak for us."
— Gerald Schwartz, *Home Planet News*

"[Kimmelman's poetry is] so seamless in its execution of form and so nuanced and unproclaimed in its delivery. . . ."
— James Tolan, *Galatea Resurrects*

"His poems are intricate and wise. . . ."
— Denise Duhamel

"The poetry of Kimmelman is precise and compact in its language, but creates vast scenery before the reader."
— Denise Bazzett, *New Pages*

"This is a carefully calibrated poetic vision filled with insights and worded with casual, unassuming grace. . . . Kimmelman's poems attest to the simple majesties of being, the massive implications of the everyday."
— Eric Hoffman, *Rain Taxi*

About the Author

Burt Kimmelman has published seven previous collections of poetry: *The Way We Live* (2011), *As If Free* (2009), *There Are Words* (2007), *Somehow* (2005), *The Pond at Cape May Point* (2002), a collaboration with the painter Fred Caruso, *First Life* (2000), and *Musaics* (1992). He has also published a number of book-length literary studies as well as scores of critical articles on medieval, modern, and contemporary poetry. In the 1980s and 1990s he was the senior editor of the now defunct *Poetry New York: A Journal of Poetry and Translation*.

Kimmelman was born and raised in New York City and now lives in a nearby suburb with his wife the writer Diane Simmons. He teaches literary and cultural studies at New Jersey Institute of Technology.

Recent interviews of Kimmelman are available online: with Tom Fink in *Jacket2* (text) and with George Spencer at *Poetry Thin Air* (video). Additional information and internet links can be found at BurtKimmelman.com.